Race Against ... Against Race

Advance Praise for *Race Against ... Against Race*

"In *Race Against ... Against Race* Sanders tells a riveting story of pushing himself to reach the goal that he thought mattered most—becoming a collegiate and professional football player. It is a gripping tale of growing up under the weightiness of segregation and poverty in the South and leaving home to go north to start life on his terms. Much of what he learned along the way is the same things that many of us come to appreciate—to value family, friends and to embrace new beginnings. In this way, Sanders pushes the reader to recall their own childhood and dreams for the future. But Sanders learned so much more in his race against race, and in the end, things work out exactly as they were meant."

—Allener M. Baker-Rogers, Ed.D.,
Retired university administrator and assistant professor of
educational researcher and co-author of *They Carried Us:
The Social Impact of Philadelphia's Black Women Leaders.*

"Although 'race' appears in the title of every chapter and topic in this book, the intense introspective by Bo-Dean Sanders is really a wonderful look at the race through life by a person who lived much of it in totally different worlds. The best part about it is to see how he is winning that race."

—Tony Leodora,
Owner TL Golf Services, host of "GolfTalk Live" radio show,
and host of the "Traveling Golfer" television program

Race Against ... Against Race is a riveting memoir that delves into the highs and lows of Bo-Dean Sanders's growth as a talented, young Black football athlete and first-generation college student, navigating identity and race. As a former Black college football athlete, this book resonated with critical moments of my life, which helped shape my identity and spearhead the launch of the National Diversity Council. I highly recommend this moving and inspiring book that you won't want to put down!"

—Dennis Kennedy,
Founder and chairman of National Diversity Council

"We have reached a once-in-a-lifetime moment—a chance to affect change—and ignite a cultural shift in the ways we view each other as human beings. One man's story might be enough to influence that change. Bo-Dean Sanders's story is at the same time both common and unique. *Race Against ... Against Race* is one read that could affect your life and those of many others.

—Marc Zumoff,
Play-by-play voice of the Philadelphia 76ers
on *NBC* Sports Philadelphia

"Bo-Dean captures the mindsets of not long ago, and even today. His story goes beyond sports, breaking down barriers to everyday lessons of reaching out, talking, and building relationships. A must-read for young and old."

—Rosa Gatti,
Retired Senior Vice President, *ESPN*

Race Against...
AGAINST RACE

My Journey of Diversity and Inclusion Through Sports

BO-DEAN SANDERS

NEW YORK

LONDON • NASHVILLE • MELBOURNE • VANCOUVER

Race Against ... Against Race

My Journey of Diversity and Inclusion Through Sports

Published in New York, New York, by Morgan James Publishing. Morgan James is a trademark of Morgan James, LLC. www.MorganJamesPublishing.com

ISBN 9781631953552 paperback
ISBN 9781631953569 eBook
ISBN 9781631953576 Case Laminate
Library of Congress Control Number: 2020947937

Cover & Interior Design by:
Christopher Kirk
www.GFSstudio.com

Morgan James is a proud partner of Habitat for Humanity Peninsula and Greater Williamsburg. Partners in building since 2006.

Get involved today! Visit
MorganJamesPublishing.com/giving-back

To my mother, Ceola.
The most powerful love between mother and son.
I miss seeing the joy and pride on her face.
To my godmother, Juanita.
I miss the guidance in her voice.

Contents

Our Unconscious Bias

definition
COMPETITION

RACE

ETHNICITY
meaning

Preface

changed and omitted the names of a few individuals in this book to protect them, not knowing their current circumstances. The content in this memoir is based on memory and conversations that are intended to convey the general idea and feel for what truly happened and said. Some words were softened to steer clear of four-letter words.

While writing this book, some of the same social (race relations) issues from the past have continued to unfold. I hope my book leaves the reader, Black and White, smarter and with the energy to think about how to build a relationship with someone from a different race.

Whenever race issues happen in our country, everyone, including the media, makes the statement, "We need to have the race conversation." I am sure that most athletes on diverse teams have already had the race conversation.

Thank you to everyone who believed in the value of this book.

Introduction

NIGHTMARE RACE

I wake up from my recurring nightmare feeling the same way I usually do in the dark of night. Depending on the time of year, I'm either in a cold or hot sweat, plagued with the feelings of fierce anxiety and downright terror. I feel my heart pounding through my chest, and I have trouble catching my breath. Wondering, "Where am I" and "what's going on?" I sense the smell of smoke, as if a church is on fire and burning to the ground. The smoke smell clouds my judgment, and I think of the Friendly Missionary Baptist Church I attended growing up in the former Confederate South. My shins hurt like someone just smacked them with a hammer, and my knees feel like a 300-pound offensive lineman just chop-blocked me. My feet are in pain, as if I have run shoeless while escaping the segregated Confederate South by way of the Underground Railroad trail while being chased by hound dogs.

When the nightmares first started, I shrugged each episode off as a bad dream, and then after the bad dreams continued, they became my nightmares. Here's how my nightmares tormented me: I'd feel miserable and tired while running in the suburbs (an affluent, predominantly White community with old Main Line money) of Philadelphia. As I continued to run, I'd think, "Why am I running?" From who or what am I running? I felt like I was running blind . . . and sadly, for my life (a Black man on the run).

I knew as a Black man running in a White, wealthy neighborhood— or in any White community—it could mean trouble or death. (I wasn't scared so I kept it moving.) I was running west, away from the big-city skyline, on Lancaster Avenue, also known as Route 30. I reached the point where I began running up the steepest incline of my race, the area of my run called "The Hill." I started my run at "The Crib." The Crib was a frat house-like place on Arthur & County Line Road, where a group of my Black classmates and friends and I lived for a little while. We were the only Blacks living on that block.

In my late-night ordeal, I am running on empty as I struggle up the hill, and I notice a police car with a White officer racing toward me. I'm not sure if the cop is from Radnor Township or the Lower Merion Police Department. My mind plays out a number of scenarios. *Did I do something wrong? Is the cop thinking that a Black boy is out of place?* But it doesn't matter to me; I am too determined and focused on making it up that dang hill. I turn to look back a few times as the "po-po" drives by, and each time I turn to look, I see my "Hood," the neighborhood where I grew up in Jacksonville, Florida. And each time I turn back around, I see something different—the old Nissan car dealership in Rosemont, a not-so-nice looking used car lot. The AM-PM gas station on the corner, a run-down building passing as a corner convenience store, is not worthy of a Wawa street sign. And across the street is a drive-thru beer, cigarette, and liquor store. I never expect to see those types of businesses on the Main Line filled with wealth, but I don't question it. I keep it moving.

I reach the Radnor House Apartments and hear voices. The voices are getting stronger, louder, closer, and then the voices become clear. Their words hit me, much like the helmet-on-helmet collisions during my football career and when coach Ferraro, my ramrod college defensive backs coach, screamed in my ear during football practice.

I hear, "Yo! Move your a** Bo-Dean, move your a**!" while an SUV and a black antique Sting Ray Corvette drive by. As the vehicles race past me, I see five people in the SUV. Frank "Happy" Dobbs, former standout college basketball player; Mr. Julius "Dr. J" Erving, 76ers great, pro basketball legend, and NBA Hall of Famer; Rich "Big Country" Lage, my former teammate; Howie Long, Oakland/LA Raider great and NFL Hall of Famer; Edward "EZ-Ed" Pinckney, 1985 NCAA Basketball Champion and the tournament's Most Outstanding Player; and in the sports car, Mr. Don DiCarlo, Sr., my one-time mentor and father figure, and Nate "Skate" Bouknight, Jr., another teammate from Norristown, PA. They are headed east on Lancaster Avenue. The only thing I can come up with is that they must be heading to Ardmore (a small town, a few miles away) for a pick-up basketball game in the park.

During my nightly moments of dream-induced agony, I'd always, finally make it up The Hill. Tonight, I am making progress and reach the halfway point. It is hot—very hot. I look up, and it is high noon. I am running in the sun. The sidewalk is narrow and hugs the road, which is typical in this area of the Main Line because the towns are old and quaint. I had run this mile before, in the winter and summer seasons, but for some reason, this run feels different. "Why is this so hard? It feels as if I am racing up the tallest hill I have ever run before. Why?"

And then it hits me as I arrive at the football stadium on campus. Today is the day I have worked hard for. The parking lot is on the left, and the football stadium towers above on the right. I see that both parking lots are at capacity. I hear both trains go by. On the right, behind the football stadium, is the Amtrak Paoli R5, and on my left, between Stanford Hall and the parking lot, is the Norristown High Speed Line. Now I know why I am running as fast and as hard as I can. I am here to graduate from college.

I arrive to see I am running behind. I am late! I have missed my college graduation ceremony. I stare at the banners and balloons, colored in blue and white and placed all around the stadium, wishing the graduates, "Congratulations!"

I have missed the part of the program where every soon-to-be graduate gets the chance to act a fool (but only a few actually try it) during the commencement. The few grads with no clue tried something outrageously stupid and original (or so they thought) but failed. Their outbursts embarrassed their families, their professors, and the deans of their academic departments. Yeah, I just missed that! It was supposed to be my big day. My celebratory day on the same football field where I smashed helmets with my teammates and our competition. But for a split second, I think maybe the ceremony was moved inside because it is blazing hot and the turf becomes excessively dangerous in the heat. It is usually hot on the turf field during this time of year (the end of May). Growing up in Florida, I hung out with my friends and played sports in heavy heat, so it didn't faze me at all.

I keep it moving. I head to the Sports Pavilion, and when I walk in the door, the gym is empty. I missed it. "What in the devil! This can't be happening to me!"

I head to the Liberal Arts Department, blood boiling, and upset because I never liked being late. I hammer my way through some of the Black and White faceless, wood-like mannequins on campus, those in their blue and white caps and gowns, to pick up my diploma. I need to see it and hold it in my hands. I need that white paper with the black ink on it. That's what I covet, need, and worked so hard to earn.

I look forward to showing my mom, family members, and friends what I earned because on my mom's immediate side of the family, I am the first male to earn a degree from college. As I continue my race to find and pick up my trophy, I pass Bartley Hall. Bartley is where I was able to (thanks to Mr. DiCarlo) eat breakfast or lunch when I was hungry and didn't have enough money in my pocket to pay for it.

I continue racing to the Liberal Arts Building, but when I get there, it isn't there—no diploma, no white paper with black ink, and no blue backdrop frame. My name isn't listed on the sign-out sheet. As a matter of fact, no one knows me. There are a few Black faces outside the building, waiting on their family members. Their faces are fuzzy, just like all the others. I say my name, and the White person on the other side of the table, the one handing out the most important document of my life, looks at me with disbelief and awkward silence, as if I don't belong there. As if a Black person, a Black student, or Black athlete should never be allowed on campus, much less earn a degree. I don't let my anger get the best of me. I remember what my mom told me, "When you lose your dang temper, your best bet is to go find it." But I feel deceived, duped, gut shot. "What did I do wrong?" This day was supposed to be the best day of my college life, the culmination of my college experience. Did I imagine the five years of hardship, hard work, achievement, and joy? Do I receive nothing? Was it a pipe dream?

My nightmares would come to end alongside the strong feeling of confusion, as I'd hear helmets smashing and the voice of my teammate, Skate, yelling, "Wake up, Bo-Dean! Wake the devil up!" Then I'd wake up.

After I gathered myself post nightmare, I'd often think, "Why do I keep having this nightmare?" Was it a hard and stressful week at work? Did I get enough sleep during the week? Did I forget to do something important, or am I suffering from the ill effects of all those helmet-on-helmet collisions during my playing days? Is my subconscious telling me something, or trying to get my attention somehow? So I'd pull myself together. I'd look for clues or any signs of any kind, any items to prove to myself that I did graduate. I needed to kill the anxiety and make sure it was just a nightmare. I'd look for that white paper with black ink, nestled in its frame on my wall (and no, it's not there).

My nightly torments haunted me for years. I was careful and focused when I looked around my place for anything to help the horrible memories and feelings go away. Before walking out of my bedroom, I'd spot, on my nightstand, my two school rings. The first was my football ring and the second, my class ring. My football ring has a blue stone with a gold *V* embedded on top, and my school ring also boasts a blue top stone with a Wild Cat logo inside. I'd then head to my living room and stop to look in my hallway closet. I find my football jerseys (one blue and the other white) with my name on the back and my jersey number—#42. I'd begin feeling better but not completely. Then, I'd find an 8½ x 11 photocopy of my diploma; it's stuffed inside one of my old school newspapers that I placed in the same spot on my black futon couch in the living room. I placed it there so that I could quickly find it the next time my nightmare happened, and it did—many, many times. When my anxiety was gone, I'd take a deep breath and turn off my TV. It was usually time to go back to bed.

My Nightmare Race continues in the Conclusion.

CHAPTER I

Starting My Race

TOPIC 1. GRADUATION RACE

I completed the first important race in my life on the day I graduated from high school, and there were some ups and downs. I graduated in 1983 from Jean Ribault High School in Jacksonville, Florida. During my graduation, the commencement speaker said, "Go out, face the world, and change the world." Minutes later, I walked across the stage in my blue & white cap and gown. My mom and the rest of my family stood proudly inside the civic arena and cheered when I walked across the stage to receive my diploma (white paper with black ink).

Outside the arena, I took pictures with my mom, sisters, godmother, grandmothers, dad, cousins, friends, and teammates. My cousin, Carol, and I were in homeroom together during our entire high school time—three years. We shared the same last name. I'm not sure how many of my teachers and classmates knew we were cousins. Our fathers—who are identical twins—were classmates with several of our teachers. I gathered with a few of my favorite teachers, football teammates, classmates, and my best friend "Jesse-Duke" Walker. It was an unforgettable night . . . and bittersweet.

The next morning, I was officially a high school graduate. And yet, to me, it was not a major achievement. But graduating from high school was viewed as an important accomplishment in my community. It was widely known that more and more Black teenage boys were dropping out of high school or not moving on to enroll in college after high school. I lived in a large Black community and my school was ninety-nine percent Black. The teachers and administrators talked to the students all the time about attending college. One of my teachers, Mrs. Vaughn, encouraged me to think about college, not as an athlete, but as a student. She taught my older sister, Pam, and had high expectations of me. Mrs. Vaughn knew that the streets were always calling young Black men, and the streets meant nothing but trouble for young Black men like me.

Playing sports in college was always the topic of conversation among athletes and my teammates. Even my classmates wanted to know who had received a scholarship to play college sports. I didn't complete the second important race in my young life. My dream of playing college football wasn't in front of me. So my heart was heavy, and my self-esteem was a little shot.

I had started playing football in junior high, and I was no different than most kids with a dream of playing college football and maybe pro. As a kid, I started seeing more Black athletes playing sports on TV. My high school head coach, Don Gaffney, was the first Black quarterback to start at the University of Florida in 1973, and that was a big deal in my community and in the South. Seeing more Black athletes participating in sports at a high-level changed everything for me. And that's the first time I remember saying, "That's what I want to be when I grow up." A football player. My high school coaches, the Gaffney brothers, (Don, Warren, and Reggie) did more than I expected to get me scouted by colleges. But I had to face reality. No major college football programs—or any college programs—offered me a scholarship or invited me to walk-on their programs. I started asking around, "Where can I get a chance to play college football?" Was it too late for me? I had doubts, and I hoped I wasn't spinning my wheels, but it felt like I was.

I had no, *what's next* or *now what* thoughts. My plan was to get a summer job at the local mall and make some money because I was going to college to earn a degree at some point. I wasn't going to be a juvenile delinquent or couch potato and develop bad habits, nor was I the type of kid that hung-out at the corner store playing video games because my mom was having none of that! I could have attended college in my hometown if I wanted to give up on playing football, but I didn't want to throw away my dream. A future playing football in Jacksonville looked bleak because there were no Division I college programs in the area. There was a junior college in town, but I didn't consider it at all—not for football—because playing for a junior college would have felt like playing high school football all over again. I followed my plan and started my first job with J.C. Penney in the men's department a few weeks after graduation.

I was excited to work and start saving some money to pay for my education. The idea of helping my mom out with a few bills around the house felt great, too. The country was fighting its way out of a recession, and my family shifted a few times up and down the fine line of lower blue-collar and poor. My mother was doing all she could to help my sister with her college expenses. My mom wanted my sister to focus on her academics. It was hard for my mother to move up the ladder of success without a college degree (and made even harder by being a Black woman). My mom didn't want that for her daughters. My sister Pamela, Pam as we call her, was a sophomore at Bethune Cookman

College (BCC), a Historically Black College founded by Mary Mcloud Bethune and located in Daytona Beach, Florida. Pam was the first of my mom's kids to go to college. I noticed how hard it was on my mom and my sister during her first two years. My brother Joseph Jr., "Jo-Jo" to us, had just finished his first year in the military, and my younger sister Cassandra, or San, was starting her senior year of high school in the fall and was a handful. My classmates, teammates, friends, and people in my neighborhood said San was a lot like me. She wasn't a lot like me; San was just like me. We were practically twins.

I knew I should have moved on with my life, but I couldn't get the feeling of not playing college football out of my system. It was the feeling of having more to give . . . if I could find the right opportunity. I didn't talk to many teammates or classmates about going to college to play football, but it was always on my mind. One of my high school teammates whom I did talk to was Reggie Northup. He was accepted to Cheyney University, a small HBCU in Pennsylvania, to play football. I didn't know anything about Cheyney. We spoke often throughout the summer as he prepared for his college football opportunity, and he knew how much I wanted to play. Reggie was a good player and a great guy. His dream came true to play college football, but my dream had been cut, like a kid trying out for a sport he had no skill to play.

As the end of summer loomed and the beginning of the fall football season began with practices around the country, not playing football hit me hard. Before Reggie left for pre-season practice and his first semester in college, he promised to keep in touch with me. Reggie made the team and kept his promise by calling me once or twice a week to talk about his college football experience. Pam and all her friends started heading back to college a few weeks later. Pam's friends attended Harvard, Cheyney, Florida A&M University (FAMU), Florida State, and others. She gave me the "big sister talk" before she headed south. She asked me to stay away from any trouble and take care of the family. Pam could see how happy I was for her to be headed back to college. And I think she knew how unhappy I was not following in her footsteps.

Later that night, my mom knew (as all moms do) something was eating at me. She asked me the only way a mother knew how: "What's wrong sweetie?"

"Every day, I see young kids walking to pre-season football practice with their equipment in hand as I sit on the bus headed to work in the mornings or on my ride back if I get off early. And seeing those players makes me think about football all day and night."

She smiled and said, "You did the best you could," but in my mind and heart, I knew I had more to give, more to do.

I daydreamed about playing college football on that bus ride to work every day. I thought about how I was going to miss the pep rallies, the bonfires at home games, homecoming, the archrival game against W.M. Raines, and traveling on the bus into hostile territory (or so we thought) to play a few games against all-White teams. I missed all of it. All of it except shaving my head into a Mohawk.

At the start of football season in the South, the excitement starts to build for the upcoming season. Football in the South had been a big deal for as long as I can remember. I grew up hearing that football in the South is our second religion, and I believed it by the time I started playing.

If my chance of playing college football was going to happen somehow or somewhere, I needed to start working out. I decided to start my next race. I trained after work and on my days off. On my days off, I'd walk to the school just up the street from my house to watch the junior high and senior high players during practice. The feelings of passion fueled me even more to work out and keep dreaming my dream. I knew I was a late bloomer because I never played Pop Warner or Pee Wee football when I was a little chocolate morsel, which meant I needed to work really hard.

TOPIC 2. HOLIDAY RACE

I continued my workouts for weeks leading up to Thanksgiving and through Christmas. Family members, co-workers, and friends constantly asked me if I missed playing football, and I admitted I did. I considered going the junior college route outside of Jacksonville, but Pam and Reggie convinced me to focus on a four-year institution. I heard stories of athletes starting their college careers late and walking-on to make a team. I was inspired by those stories, one after the other, and I heard those stories more often during the holiday season, while the bowl games filled our TV screens.

Although the holiday season was an exciting time for sports, I couldn't help but feel it was getting close to the time when I would need to make a decision about my future. In most people's eyes, my chances of playing college football were non-existent, I had no shot—don't even think about it. It wasn't going to happen. The window was starting to close for me. In my heart and mind, my hopes and dreams of playing were becoming my nightmare. It was a wonderful dream while it lasted, but my dream started to look like it wasn't realistic. As the time passed and the days moved further and further away from graduation, I was no closer to living my dream of going to college to play football than seeing a Black man named "B.O." becoming president of the United States.

The night my sister returned home from college was a good night. It was the official start of my family's holiday season and Christmas break for college students. I walked into a house full of women. My mom, San, and most of Pam's best friends (Tammy and Brenda were like sisters to me) were sitting in the family room. I smiled when I saw Pam, and we exchanged hugs. I sat and listened to my sister and her best friends talk about the semester. My sister was very smart, and I knew she didn't have any problems with her academics. She asked me if I still wanted to go to college.

"Yes, that's why I'm still working out."

"Have you heard from Reggie?"

"Yes, we talk all the time."

My mom was in the kitchen making her lunch for work the next day. She asked, "How was work today?"

I replied, "I had a good day and I sold two suits."

"You look good in your suit, sweetie. You don't see many Black men going to work in suits around here, only to church." I smiled and gave her a kiss.

The Christmas-time weather in Jacksonville varied from warm to cold. Most Southerners feel that if it's below seventy degrees, it's cold. Days before Santa "rode in" to bring smiles to every little boy and girl who'd been naughty, nice, or downright spoiled is also the same time when college students come home and show off. It's always the most wonderful time of the year. Most college students are home and ready to hang out; they soon head out to the holiday parties with all their high school friends. Some use that opportunity to rub their successful college experience in the faces of the "frenemies" they left behind.

Instead, I looked forward to Reggie coming home because he had kept his promise of keeping in contact with me while at Cheyney. He usually called me on Saturday nights after a game or on Sunday nights. I looked forward to seeing faces I hadn't seen in a while. Faces I hadn't seen since my high school graduation. More than a few of my high school classmates went off to college. They were home for Christmas break and talking about their college experiences, but I wouldn't be able to add to that conversation. More girls in my high school and neighborhood attended college as compared to the guys. So there would be more girls to check out at the parties. And I got the chance to hang out with my former teammate and classmates.

A few nights after Christmas, I returned home from work, and my sister was already out with her friends. I quickly changed into my workout clothes, walked out the door, and headed for the street in front of our house. I got my short workout in and went back in the house since it was a little cold that night. I turned on the TV to catch the late local sports highlights that I had missed the night before. It was college football bowl time and holiday basketball tournament season. I looked forward to watching the Gator Bowl game between the Florida Gators vs. Iowa Hawkeyes, coming up in a couple of days.

But that night, I happened to catch the highlights of my hometown Jacksonville University's (JU Dolphins) Christmas Basketball Tournament. I also caught the highlights of the Auburn University basketball team kicking some school's gluteus maximus. The sports anchor described one of the players from Auburn; I didn't catch his name at that moment, but I remember seeing the highlights showing this (as we would say in the South: big-boned, country boy from off the farm) dunking and slamming the ball on and all over the other team. It wasn't unusual to see a big, heavy kid in the South playing basketball. However, it was unusual to see a kid that size jump out of the building with the combination of force and leaping ability. It was one dunk after the other, another rebound and a dunk, and all of his dunks were *take that*, *have some*, or *in your face* trash talk highlight dunks. He earned a new nickname after every dunk. It wasn't a wonderful time of year for the other team because that big boy was a nightmare to play against. He ruined the other team's Christmas tournament. He basically beat the other team all on his own and put them in "Boot Hill." That Auburn player carried his team to victory.

I remember the sports anchor referring to the losing team as the Wildcats. I noticed the school's team colors were blue and white, which was cool because they were the same colors as my junior and senior high schools'. Other than that, there was no reason to remember the losing team. I didn't watch college basketball as much as I watched football, but after what I saw, I looked for that "big country bumpkin, off the farm" kid's sport's highlights every chance I got. Once I decided to keep an eye out for that oversized donut in the SEC, it gave me another reason to follow Auburn. I liked Auburn because my mom was born in Atmore, Alabama but raised in Mobile, and we had family there. And the other reason was Bo Jackson, the all-American running back. Jackson was the top running back in the country, and we shared similar nicknames.

TOPIC 3. DREAM RACE

The dream of playing big-time, Division I (D-I) college football had come true for a few of my teammates. And when they committed and signed their letters of intent to Boston College and Central Florida, my coaches, teammates, teachers, and classmates were happy for them. Everyone knew where my teammates were headed for college, and I knew I was heading . . . nowhere. I had a spotty football career, but I was the "tough kid with potential" (my coaches called it), and I needed more experience. I needed more training, time to develop, and time to grow because I was a late bloomer. I improved by working hard during the off-seasons and the summers leading up to the football seasons. But at the end of my sophomore season, I was moved from defense to offense because my coaches said that's where the team needed me. I accepted my role, but I was playing out of position, and I knew my dream of earning a scholarship to play on defense as a defensive back (strong or free safety) was more than likely over.

I received three introduction letters before I graduated: two for football—from the University of Illinois and the University of South Carolina—and one for baseball from Rollins College. I only played one game of high school baseball because the running backs coach (Reggie Gaffney), who also coached baseball, needed one more person to field a team for the day. I wanted to help, and I did. Then I quit. That was the only time I'd ever quit anything in my life. Again, coach Gaffney said, "I had potential." But I didn't really see it as quitting because I never wanted to play baseball. Forget the fact that it was boring to watch on TV.

With those experiences in my rear-view mirror, it fueled me every day to work hard. My workouts in front of the house at night after work were different than my workouts on the track during the day at my high school. On my off days, I worked out for hours. I included basketball as part of my routine at the elementary school, next to my high school, and then I walked over to my high school, to run sprints on the open grass (our practice field). Then, I'd go on the football field and simulate playing defensive back during a football game. I wanted to play defensive back, not offensive tackle or wide receiver. I assumed the positions of strong safety and free safety. I practiced a number of defensive plays (cover 2, 3, or man) and finished with a run on the track, Then, I would do it all over again until it was time to head home. And it was time to go home when the streetlights came on.

I lived in a single-family home (not in public housing, the projects, or the ghetto) miles from downtown Jacksonville, and it was a safe neighborhood for a long time. However, things started to change in the early '80s. My neighborhood was a working-class area and wasn't crime-ridden. But drive-by shootings were starting to become something I heard about in other Black neighborhoods on the news. Getting caught in the crossfire seemed to happen to a lot of innocent people the news reported, and every now and then, those people would be athletes. I saw the agony on those mother's faces, and I didn't want my mom to be one of those moms.

In high school, my mom wanted me home when the streetlights came on because the streets were starting to chew up and spit out young Black men. My mom was very strict with me. So I did my best to stick to her streetlight rules if I wasn't at work. But that wasn't true for a few of the young Black men in my neighborhood. Some of the Black kids hung out up the street at the corner store and under the streetlights. They didn't do much, just killed time.

Over time, I noticed that killing time at the corner store and under the streetlights caught up with them. I was focused on my workouts. Part of my workout routine at night, after I returned home from work, was running wind sprints and shuttle runs to increase my speed and quickness. I did as many wind sprint reps as I could—until my legs hurt or more than hurt. They felt like they were burning and on fire.

I started my home workouts sprinting from the telephone pole in front of my house and racing to the pole at the end of my next-door neighbor's house. You could fit two small houses between the phone poles. On those nights when I got home a little early from work, my mom and godmother, Juanita Barnes (who lived across the street), would check on me. Sometimes, I changed my workout routine if I had a busy shift at work, ripping and running around the store, and had been on my feet all day. I'd sprint half the distance from the beginning of my drive-way to the end of my godmother's driveway, which was thirty yards.

My mom and dad had been divorced for years, and it was a coinci-dence that his second family lived around the corner. (My second family of siblings included my baby sister Alicia and her sisters Michelle and Yolanda.) It wasn't that complicated to understand for people from a divorced family. Sometimes my dad would drive by and see me work-ing out; he was a night owl. We'd have very short conversations—we weren't close—and then I'd get back to working out.

New Year's Eve had come and gone but the department store was still busy. I continued to work many late hours. When I got home, it would be a little late for my mom because she got up early for work every morning. So I would stick my head in her door to let her know I was home. If she weren't sound asleep, I would give her a kiss good night. She tried to stay up until I got home on those late nights. My sister, San, would also be in bed asleep, with her dog, Chico. That dog would be lying at the foot of her bed protecting her as if he was guarding the Queen of Egypt.

On those really late nights, I tried to keep my grunting and other noises during my workouts down to a minimum. I was careful not to wake my mom or godmother because they were hardworking Black women (not welfare queens), who got up early every morning and their rest was important. As far as my safety was concerned, I wasn't afraid of any potential danger lurking around the corner or coming down the street. I got my workout done and called it a night. Every day, I reminded myself why I was working out. My dream was to get to college and play football. I wanted to be ready if the opportunity came my way. So I kept dreaming and working out.

It was a week after New Year's in 1984 when it happened. I came home from work and my mom, Juanita, Pam, San, Reggie, and Carl were standing in the living room. Almost everyone who had encouraged me to keep dreaming was there except my best friend, Jesse-Duke. He had been my best friend since junior high and was absent because we had started to drift apart. The streets got him and weren't letting go, and he was hanging out with the wrong crowd. After high school, it was as if he had dropped off the face of the earth.

I thought everyone was there to say goodbye to Reggie and Carl, and they were waiting on me to get home so I could see Reggie before they headed back to Cheyney. But as it turned out, I was leaving with them. Without me knowing it, Juanita, Pam, and Carl (the student class president at Cheyney University) had been working on getting me into college behind the scenes. My guess is that Reggie helped as well. Carl, Reggie, and Pam gave me the news: I had been accepted into Cheyney University. I was headed to college in the morning with Carl and Reggie. My hopes and dreams had become a reality. I didn't choose Cheyney. Cheyney chose me. My family and friends had moved heaven and earth to get me into college. Everything I worked hard for was coming true. I was thrown a lifeline, and now my life had new meaning.

CHAPTER II

Traveling Race

TOPIC 4. SOUTHERN CONFEDERATE RACE

And just like that, I was headed to college. As I saw it, I started my official race to play college football. It was hard for me to explain or express to everyone how I felt because I didn't know how. I did the only thing I knew how to do. I thanked Carl more than once, kissed my mom, hugged my sisters, embraced my godmother, and gave Reggie the "cool brother handshake," while keeping an eye on my mom. I will never forget the excitement and pride on her face.

After discussing our travel plans, everyone headed back to their houses. I thanked Carl again before he pulled out of our driveway. I wanted to leave as soon as I had received the news. So I asked Pam, "When are we leaving?" My sister smiled at my hyped up excitement. She quickly calmed me down and then sat me down for a heart-to-heart.

Pam, my mom, and my godmother were concerned about us (three young Black men) being on the road overnight. It was no secret that trouble could find Black men at night. So the best thing to do when traveling that distance was to limit or avoid possible roadblocks, barriers, and any unforeseen issues. I took her to mean, we needed to avoid any back-wooded, White supremacists and the Ku Klux Klan, or KKK. No one wanted us driving through the former Southern Confederate states at night. So Carl planned to pick me up around 6:00 a.m.

San helped me pack as Pam continued with the older sister talk. She talked about focusing on my studies, representing our family in the right way, avoiding trouble, making wise decisions, and learning about Black history. I'm not too proud to say I was more than a little naïve about the whole starting college process and the traveling challenges. I had no clue what to expect. I didn't know much about Cheyney University, other than what my sister and Reggie told me. I knew Cheyney was an HBCU, but I didn't know its history. Heck! I didn't remember filling out the school's application during my senior year. I think I did it just to get Pam off my back. My dream was to play big time football in the SEC. I never dreamed of a team up north. Call it youthful ignorance, but it was my window of opportunity, and I was happy to have it. I trusted Pam's, Carl's, Reggie's, and Juanita's joint decision for me to attend Cheyney. I would have to fill in the other blanks as I went along.

All I could think about was that I was heading to college, and I was going to do everything I could once I got there to make the team and play. I was too excited to sit still, so I asked if there was anything my mom needed me to do around the house. If so, it was done. I walked across the street to my godmother's house and asked her the same question. She said, "No" and gave me another big hug. "Just do your best."

I didn't have much to take with me, but I checked my travel bag a few times. I had taken a green military duffle bag that my brother had left behind, and I made sure I packed my high school memory book.

I couldn't sleep. My mind raced a mile a minute. I couldn't slow my mind down from thinking about what was happening. I finally sat on the couch to watch the news in the living room. I didn't want to miss Carl's headlights when he pulled in the driveway, not sure if he would ring the doorbell or knock on the front door. I remember thinking, "My football opportunity is up north in the Philadelphia, Pennsylvania area, and that's where the Eagles and Sixers play." I wasn't an Eagles fan at all; I was a Dallas Cowboys fan, but I was a fan of Dr. J and the 76ers. *Who wasn't?* I didn't know what college football was like for Black athletes up north, but I did know Black athletes had to play football at Black colleges in the South and in other parts of the country for a long time because White schools wouldn't accept or recruit Black athletes.

I fell asleep for a few hours on the couch, and then Carl's headlights hit the front windows of my house just before the sun started to rise. I heard my mom's alarm clock and then my sister's. I was ready when Carl arrived. I said goodbye to San and her dog. Pam started a conversation with Carl as I put my things in his car. I kissed my mother goodbye as she gave me the important, albeit quick, motherly talk.

"When things get hard, remember what you learned in church. Remember what I taught you, and be strong." And then it was time for me to go. I caught her wiping the tears from her eyes as we drove away. I'd never forget it.

I didn't get the chance to tell my co-workers, friends from the neighborhood, high school teammates, classmates, extended family members, or high school coaches the good news. I didn't get the chance to say goodbye. My sisters and mom assured me they would tell everybody. It was as if I had vanished.

We picked Reggie up next, and then we headed to I-95 North. I was the new guy with less experience traveling on this long road trip, so I was more than happy to sit in the back seat, excited and anxious. I was bright-eyed and full of energy. I couldn't thank Carl and Reggie enough at the start of our trip. I didn't want to ask too many questions, so I sat back, listening to the guys talk while daydreaming and enjoying the view. I started to think about all the conversations Reggie and I had leading up to that point and all the hard work—the blood, sweat, and tears—I had put into my workouts.

As we passed Fernandina Beach—quietly referred to as the Black beach in the Black community—memories surfaced of the great holiday events (Memorial Day, 4th of July, and Labor Day) where my family went to barbeque on the beach, I learned to swim, and Black folks enjoyed time away from home.

As a young kid traveling to the beach one time, one of my siblings asked my mom, as we drove by Jacksonville Beach, "Why do we need to drive forty-five minutes or more to Fernandina Beach when the other beaches are closer to our house?" Funny thing, I was thinking the same question.

My mom replied, "That's the way it is, baby." As a kid, the friendly or Southern interaction between Blacks and Whites in the Jacksonville area was awkward and uncomfortable, depending on where you lived. If my family went shopping on the other side of the river, the segregated White side or predominantly White side of town, some Whites engaged with our Southern hospitality by saying, "Hello," and others would not. You knew where you stood if you were Black.

Just before we approached the Florida-George state line, I realized this was my second time traveling out of the state, and this trip would be longer. I was leaving the state where my life began and where I had lived for eighteen years, the place where everyone born and raised is described as having a laid-back personality and walked at a slower pace, and where the weather was great eighty percent of the time. The place where I could walk a few blocks to go crabbing or fishing; where I could find a fruit tree in less than a minute; where the Southern country style and soul food is to die for; where I could play outside sports pretty much year-round or go adventure-seeking in the swamps or woods; where the lower middle class or low-income folks went shopping at the flea-markets; and where Disney World was two hours in the southwest direction.

After we entered Georgia, a.k.a. "The Peach State," I really got pumped up. I couldn't help but think about the 39th President of the United States, Jimmy Carter, the peanut farmer. Most Blacks in my neighborhood and at church thought President Carter was a good president and a very nice White man. My mom told me she voted for the peanut farmer, and if I could've voted for him, I think I would have, too. I spied the *Welcome to Georgia* sign and a rest stop, the first of many rest stops and welcome signs I looked forward to seeing as I traveled through the former Southern Confederate States.

TOPIC 5. MIGRATING RACE

Our plan was to drive straight through every state and only stop for gas, food, and to use the men's room. I began checking out the roadside mileage markers, billboards, and eventually the signposts with the cities and small towns coming up. As we made our way through Georgia, I marveled at all sorts of cities and towns, some small and a few a little larger. I'd check out the skyline or see no skyline. I looked left and right to find hotels, motels, and Holiday Inns that attracted tired or vacationing travelers.

I counted the number of fast-food restaurants, major hotels, and gas stations as we passed the many exit ramps. The iconic McDonald's *M* dominated the I-95 landscape, but I was more of a Burger King and Krystal's kid. I asked the guys if there was a Krystal's burger joint near the school, and they replied, "No, but there is something like it called White Castle, but it's nowhere near Cheyney." It was easy to stay awake during the drive since I was bright-eyed by the newness and full of excitement to get to the next city or town.

I was interested in finding out what music each city or town was listening to. It was hard to find an R&B radio station, so we surfed the radio waves until we found something we liked. I loved all types of music, including country music from James Taylor. At one point, one of the guys skipped over one of my favorite songs by The Charlie Daniels Band called "Devil Went Down to Georgia." I didn't want the guys to know I liked country music, so I didn't say anything.

As we drove through the former Confederate South, for some reason, I found myself from time to time looking for cotton fields, sugarcane farms, or any other kind of farm that Blacks from the South fled to seek and find freedom in the North. In both the front and back of my mind, I knew we were traveling through the once legally segregated South, one that held a racist and violent past. I had learned and understood the history of the Confederate South in church and in school. It was well documented. Millions of Black Americans migrated north for a better life, an education, and work opportunities. Now, I was in a position to migrate north for my own hopes and dreams. At that moment, I tried to imagine how millions of Blacks felt traveling to the North to take advantage of opportunity. I thought about my grandmother and her decision to remain in the South.

My grandmother didn't migrate north to Detroit from Mobile like a few of her siblings had done because she had met her husband and moved to Jacksonville. Millions of Black Americans migrated north to escape the actions and culture of Southern White people who opposed the advancement of Black Americans. The southern states where Jim Crow laws, or as I've named the practice, "James Coward's laws," consisting of blatant, blunt racist attitudes and actions were alive and well after the Jim Crow laws became illegal. But their resentment and resistance to the Civil Rights movement continued in overt, subtle, and ignorant ways.

As we continued traveling through the Dixieland South, I thought about *The Green Book*, or officially titled, *The Negro Motorist Green Book*, published by Vincent Hugo Green. I had heard my grandmother, her church friends, and elders around me talk about it over the years. My grandmother was an usher at our Southern Baptist church. On Sundays, I heard church members talk about the book from time to time. If there was a conversation about someone traveling, mention of *The Green Book* always followed. Some called the book, "The Black Bible for Traveling." The Black community used the book to avoid White hatred, bigotry, discrimination, and possible death while Black folks traveled in and across the United States for many years. The *Green Book* was created by a Black man for Black families traveling to visit family members, Black business travelers, or Black athletes and Black teams traveling from city to city for competition.

Was I confident we would not run into any issues? No. But Carl had made the trip many times before and was road-tested. He was smart, and his understanding of Black history was useful during our trip. Carl, Reggie, and I were not a rowdy bunch, so there was very little reason to be overly concerned about getting stopped by the po-po (local police) or 5-0 (state troopers) other than DWB. Driving While Black was always out there, pecking or lurking around the corner of an old unworked farm or cotton field as we traveled through the Southern states.

The last thing we needed was a yellowbelly KKK member with a badge and masquerading as a police officer, looking to violate our civil rights by stopping us or worse because we were three Black college students from another state driving through "his" town, city, state, or "his America." I witnessed cars racing by with a group of Black people, a group of White people, and a few cars with Blacks and Whites traveling together. I thought to myself, those Black folks are taking a chance by putting the pedal to the metal. As we continued to travel north, if we saw a police car with its emergency (red and blue) lights on, it got our attention and that meant someone was pulled over. I looked to see if that person was Black or White. If the person in the car was Black, a prayer for their safety followed. Carl was a serious guy who followed the laws and the unwritten rules for Blacks who were traveling. And without a doubt, Reggie and I followed his lead.

I was too excited to be scared while driving through the former Antebellum South, but I was still cautious. We were careful whenever stopping at a rest stop or gas station to get something to eat in any small town. We paid close attention to our surroundings. Did I see any blatant symbols of hate or White supremacy? No! I never saw what I learned about in school or in Sunday School—the "Blacks and Whites only" signs on restroom doors or the separate drinking fountains at rest stops.

We were never refused service at the gas stations and no racial slurs were spoken. We pumped our gas, used the restrooms, paid for something to eat, and we moved on. There was no time to rub noses with a few potential racist people.

It wasn't blatant. But in some places, I could feel the hate. When we stopped, the plan was to get it all done at the same time. "One-stop pop" we called it, pop in and pop out. One of us would keep an eye on the car and pay for the gas while getting something to eat, another would pump the gas, and the third would hit the men's room. We rotated during our next stop.

Our goal was to get to Cheyney without any trouble. The Antebellum South wasn't the Jim Crow South. But the Civil Rights Act of 1964 wasn't too far removed from 1984, and we understood that. Twenty years didn't seem like a long time for us and with that kind of history in our rearview mirror (caution, objects in the rearview mirror are closer than they appear), twenty years was closer than we wanted it to be.

TOPIC 6. INTERSTATE 95 RACE

As we approached big cities, the traffic got heavy. Sometimes, I missed the smaller ghost towns with blowing dust and tumbleweeds because we'd be in and out of them in a jiffy. To race through small towns and cities could mean trouble for us and did mean trouble for Blacks in the past. We continued traveling with caution because we weren't looking for any trouble, and we didn't want trouble finding us. We were in the heart of the South, but I wasn't scared. In my life, I had experienced gang fights, and I lived through having a gun put to my head with the finger on the trigger. I'd seen violence up close and none of it came from the "White Man" but that didn't mean he wasn't out there waiting for us.

I recognized the names of a few of the big cities and attractions, such as South of the Border. I had heard about this particular tourist trap from classmates, friends, and even on TV. I heard it was easy to recognize by its big sombrero. Driving from Florida to Pennsylvania was going to be a long, twelve-hours-plus ride if we followed the speed limit, so from time to time, Carl would ask Reggie to drive. I didn't get mad when he didn't ask me. It was likely based on my driving record. And Carl and I had some history between us.

During the summer of 1982, I had asked my mom to use her car. "Betsy the Bonneville" was the name my mom called her car (a pre-owned Pontiac Bonneville). My mother spent time with me, trying to teach me to drive when I was ready to get my license, and when she couldn't take it anymore, she asked my Uncle Joe to teach me. She let me use her car to go to the mall to pick up the sports items I needed for summer football practice. She cautiously said, "Yes," but specifically told me not to give anyone a ride home or go joy riding with anybody from the mall.

"Ok, mom," and then I totally disobeyed her wishes.

I ran into my best friend from the neighborhood, Jesse-Duke. He needed a ride home from the mall, and I told him I would take him. Jesse lived a few blocks up the street from me. It started to rain while we were inside the mall, but the rain quickly stopped—typical Florida weather. It wasn't uncommon to get hit with rain for a minute or two. Then, the sun would reappear again and dry up the wet tears that Mother Nature would sometimes turn into a river stream.

On the way home, I decided to avoid the main traffic and take the back roads. I thought it was the safest way to go. The back roads were curvy and had less traffic. Just before we reached our neighborhood, I hit a wet spot, lost control, and the car hydroplaned. My uncle taught me how to handle a car when you hit a wet spot, and thankfully, I remembered. I quickly regained control, but in the end, I hit a large flower bush that stopped me from driving into the river. The river was to my right and houses were to my left. Jessie and I got out of the car and he said, "You weren't going fast."

I looked at him in disbelief and said, "Yes, I was!"

We both took a look around the car to see if there was any damage. There was none. However, the car was stuck in the muddy grass leading into the river, and the house across the street, from where we had slid, sported tire track marks in their front yard. Unfortunately, I had damaged or destroyed a few of the flower plants in the yard when the car swerved from left to right. It was just my luck. Not only did I damage someone's property, but it was Carl's parents' claim. Out of all the properties to have a car accident, it had to be my sister's friend from the neighborhood. That was the first time I had officially met Carl and his parents. What a bad first impression to leave.

My reminiscing of the accident ended. We finally reached North Carolina, and I briefly thought about my first trip outside the state of Florida. When I was in high school, I was nominated and received the Fellowship of Christian Athletes Award. I was nominated by my high school coaches, the Gaffney brothers, because I had made a team sacrifice (switching from defense to offense). As the FCA award winner, I represented my high school football team in the North Carolina mountains during a weeklong summer camp. The camp focused on leadership, athletic skills, and social development. Also, the camp's mission was to prepare young athletes for future competition and sportsmanship.

As we traveled through Virginia, I noticed a few signs that read, *Virginia is for Lovers,* and I wondered, "Lovers of what?" But it didn't matter because I knew we were getting closer to Pennsylvania.

I started to get excited again as we reached the Maryland Welcome Center. There was snow on the ground, and the sight of it was amazing and beautiful. I had never seen that much snow in my life. I'd seen flurried in Jacksonville once every six to eight years. The flakes would never stick. By the time the flurries hit the grass, they turned to water. My journey had officially taken me to a place where I could see mountains of snow (what it looked like to me); the feeling was wonderful, but the temperature was dreadful. The longer we traveled north, the colder it grew, and by the time we reached Delaware, it was darn cold.

When we finally reached Pennsylvania, crossing the border of the Mason-Dixon Line, and then arrived at Cheyney University, it was downright crazy-freezing cold, and I knew I wasn't going to like Mother Nature's winter or father Hawk blowing wind at all.

I-95 was the main interstate connecting me to each state and what a wonderful experience it was traveling up north. I'd have a story to tell when I got back home. Our long road trip was racist free and made possible by the sacrifices of so many people who created the path for the Black Americans. We drove from state to state, starting with Florida, and moving through Georgia, South Carolina, North Carolina, Virginia, Maryland, and Delaware to get to Cheyney, Pennsylvania. I wasn't escaping, fleeing, or running away from something. I was migrating north to chase my dream of playing college football. My world was changing. It wasn't because of something I had done; it was because of something people had done for me, and I wasn't going to disappoint them. I was going to take full advantage of the opportunity and blessing. I truly didn't know what the campus experience would be like, but I assumed it would be like my high school or my neighborhood, and I was willing to learn—to just go with it. I would be on the campus of the nation's oldest Black educational institution. So I assumed the entire Cheyney community was Black.

CHAPTER III

Cheyney Race

TOPIC 7. MOVING-IN RACE

I arrived on the campus of Cheyney University in January 1984, early in the evening. Knock on wood, we didn't run into any barriers or road-blocks, and we didn't face any discrimination driving through the former Southern Confederate states. It was pitch black and unbearably cold as we approached the campus. I didn't see much of the local area, but what I did see was farmland and a lot of Christmas lights on the single-family homes in the area. I thought to myself, "Cheyney is out in the boonies!" Snow was on the ground—mountains of it. I'd never seen so much white stuff in my life. I couldn't help but think, "That's a ton of snow!" The snow looked like the sand dunes I had played on at the beach as a kid.

Carl took a victory lap around the campus to celebrate our safe arrival and to give me a quick overview of the campus. He drove up to the front of the men's dormitory and parked the car, pointing out where I would be living—where all of the male students lived. Cheyney had one male and one female dorm. We got out of the car, fetched our bags, and walked through the front doors. It was my first time in a college dorm, and I was so pumped up. I was playing it cool and trying not to show it. I wanted to go to my room right away. There was a security guard at the front desk who knew Carl. Carl pointed to me and told the guard I'm a new freshman. The guard allowed us the time we needed to move in. Carl's room was on the first floor, and he was the Residence Hall Rep.

We took the stairs to the second floor because the elevator was in use. Carl walked me to my room and introduced me to a few guys walking the halls as they had returned from their Christmas break and were moving back in, as well. We got to my room and Carl gave me the key. I open the door to my room and walked in. The room was empty. My roommate hadn't shown up yet. I had no anxiety about sharing a room because I had shared a bedroom with my brother my entire life, at least until he had joined the military. I placed my things on a bed, looked around the room, took a deep breath, and thought, "I made it."

Reggie's room was across the hall. I walked down the hall to find the phone, call my mom, and let her know we had made it safe and sound. She asked if my room was okay, and I told her it was perfect. She apologized for not having the money to buy a TV to send with me to college.

"Don't worry about it. Maybe my roommate will have one; besides, I have my radio." I could hear in her voice that she felt at ease and my confidence put her at ease. Next, I talked to Pam and complained about the cold weather. She said, "You'll be alright," but I wasn't sure. She was ready to head back to BCC. I was lucky to have my older sister with her college experience to walk me through my start. She gave me the big sister talk again—more about focusing on my schoolwork and if I had any problems, go to Carl, and he would help me out.

After Carl and Reggie unpacked, we took a quick walk around campus. They pointed out where I needed to be for registration, orientation, and then they took me to the Athletic Department, where the coach's offices were located. I wasn't prepared for the way the cold air went through my clothes. I had the wrong shoes for the winter snow. As a matter of fact, I had no snow boots or winter clothes at all. I had a pair of jeans and more than enough pairs of sweats. I quickly learned that Cheyney's campus was small enough to walk to class without a heavy jacket, but that didn't help with my mental adjustment to the cold weather in this region called the Northeast. After a quick evaluation, I decided I didn't like the cold weather.

I spent my first night getting settled in. The feeling I had was more than excitement; it was a joy and a blessing. I turned my radio on and was able to find an R&B radio station, which played great music. I didn't feel out of place or as if I was on my own. I looked forward to the next day and everything that would come with it. I never had an official visit to Cheyney with my mom while in high school, but it didn't matter. It felt like home, and I was there to stay.

The next morning more students showed up. I could hear them moving into their rooms. My roommate arrived, and I didn't know if it was a coincidence or if it was planned, but he was from Florida and a member of the football team. After we talked, I knew we'd get along fine. Reggie dropped in to welcome my roommate back and to personally introduce me as his homie and high school teammate. They exchanged Christmas break stories, talking about their families and the holiday bowl games. Then, it was time for me to meet the coaches.

Students were moving around the campus as we walked to the coaches' offices. The Black culture and environment weren't new to me, so I didn't worry about fitting in. It was my second tour of the campus in twenty-four hours, and I was able to finally see the residence halls, classroom buildings, and other facilities under the bright light of the sun. The campus was beautiful. I met the head coach and a few of the position coaches. The head coach and I spoke for a few minutes. He gave me his expectations and asked about my family. It was my first official conversation with a college football coach, and it felt good. He seemed very interested in where I came from and in my future. He said, "We could use you if you compete like Reggie and you're not a troublemaker. I see no reason why you can't make it on the team and help us win games." The coach said everything I wanted to hear and more. But I knew I still had to prove myself in spring practice, and I planned to do just that.

TOPIC 8. ORIENTATION RACE

My freshman orientation class was small. I had missed the larger freshman incoming class five months earlier. I didn't feel out of place because I learned that Cheyney offered kids like me a chance to attend college. Everyone in my orientation class was just like me in one way or the other (a late bloomer or needed a fresh start). Each student had a story of challenges they had to overcome just to get to Cheyney. Some needed to work and save money before they could attend college, a few needed to finish high school, some needed to get their lives straight, and two transferred in from other universities. I was at Cheyney because it was my only legit opportunity.

I arrived at Cheyney at the right time. Enrollment was very high, and tuition and room and board were affordable using grants and loans. That made it easier for me and other students who qualified but had to go it alone without their parents help or students whose parents did what they could to help by offsetting the cost of their education. Cheyney's flexible admission rules opened doors for students like me with hopes and dreams, but more importantly, Cheyney was able to answer the prayers of my mother and so many other mothers who had hopes and dreams for their children.

I sat in orientation, focused on making a good impression, paying attention, and participating. I wanted to complete the first part of my college experience, and I looked forward to learning more about Cheyney. Cheyney was founded in 1837 and was located in Cheyney, PA, about twenty miles from Philadelphia. I learned the history of Cheyney University and the sacrifices generations of Black Americans made in the past. And over time, Cheyney was open to educating students from all walks of life—Black, White, and other. If a student couldn't afford to attend a more expensive college or university in the city or the state, Cheyney was an option. Plus, Cheyney provided a few special academic programs that other schools didn't offer.

Cheyney had its notable alumni and trailblazers, one being Philadelphia's own Ed Bradly of "60 Minutes." Bradly was the only Black person on *CBS*'s "60 Minutes" program. I didn't watch the show regularly, but from time to time during the NFL season, I would catch Ed Bradly on Sunday nights after watching a game. Sometimes, the "60 Minutes" program would start immediately after the Dallas Cowboys had beaten the Philadelphia Eagles or another NFL team.

When it came to Cheyney's sports programs, I was all ears. Cheyney's football program was dealing with a string of unsuccessful years. I remember wishing I was on campus at the start of the year to experience the football season and all the events leading up to homecoming. Homecoming was big at my sister's school and at most, if not all, of the HBCUs in the country. I wasn't sure how Cheyney's homecoming would compare. The men's and women's basketball programs had a strong history. Cheyney won the 1978 Division II National Basketball Championship, coached by John Chaney, who had left a few years earlier to coach the Temple Owls' men's basketball team and C. Vivian Stringer, coached the women's basketball team before moving on.

Attending the orientation class allowed me to reflect on my upbringing as the instructor reviewed the rules and what was expected from each student. Growing up and attending a Southern Baptist Church, learning good values and the basic understanding of right from wrong, helped me adjust just fine. Also, going to Sunday School before church helped me develop a sense of discipline and the fear of doing something that was not allowed. I learned to go to school and not miss class.

Cheyney was an ideal university because of its HBCU identity, a few of my standout classmates, and its longstanding Black power efforts in educating young Blacks living in America. Most of the students felt obligated to attend Cheyney because of the school's HBCU identity. Others felt the need to continue their family's legacy because their father, mother, older sibling, or someone in their family graduated from Cheyney. For some, it was their dream of living out that HBCU experience and graduating from an HBCU institution.

My classmates came from Black neighborhoods in Philadelphia and cities or towns in the surrounding area, such as Coatesville, Norristown, Upper Darby, and Chester. Cheyney attracted students from all over the country, as well. Many were from neighboring states—New Jersey, Delaware, the five boroughs in New York, Maryland, and Washington, D.C.—in addition to other states along the east coast . . . and of course, from as far south as Florida.

TOPIC 9. DATING RACE

I had walked onto Cheyney's campus with one goal in mind: to walk-on and make the football team in spring practice. It was time to leave my high school experiences (good or bad) behind. Falling in love wasn't on my mind. I avoided dating in high school, and I wasn't interested in a serious relationship after I graduated. I was only interested in football and the steps it took to help me get to the next level. I had heard all I needed to hear from family members and teachers about the pitfalls of serious dating at a young age. And how it could change your life if you're not careful and not focused on graduating from high school.

I had the best defensive moves to keep the girls away while in high school. My first line to anyone who wanted to get close to me was that my sisters were always checking up on me by calling the girl's house and asking her a whole bunch of questions, and if that didn't slow her down, I would tell her, "The only woman I could ever love is my mother," and then she would run for the hills. That was my adolescent way of avoiding all dating situations and my way of saying I was too preoccupied to be interested in dating.

Now, don't get me wrong I had a crush on a few girls, but it was only puppy love. One attended my grandmother's church; one visited her family member in my neighborhood from time to time; and one attended my high school. But it never went anywhere, because the time and energy involved would have been blocking my dream of playing football, and football always won out.

After a week of college orientation, I began to get my feet on solid ground. I started to settle in, and I guess I let my guard down. College created the perfect atmosphere for me to start dating, and dating in college was much harder to avoid. I didn't see it coming. When you fall for someone, it can shift your focus, plans, and entire path. I heard it said, "Love is where you find it," and love found me when I wasn't looking for it. I fell with no real dating experience and that meant I was wet behind the ears.

I was more than smitten with her. I fell head-over-heels with a class-mate in orientation. Something magical happened when I first saw her, and I couldn't take my eyes off her. She was beautiful, sophisticated, walked with confidence, and had an independent spirit. I was tied in knots every time she walked past me. It hit me like the feeling you get when you hear a beautiful love song by Marvin Gaye that comes across the radio airwaves late at night.

I fell for a woman who was no ordinary freshman. She was a few years older than me and from the Bronx, New York. She started college after her marriage didn't work out. She wasn't friendly at first, but that didn't hold me back. I was able to get her to smile with a little Southern charm.

I said to her, "In the south when someone makes eye contact and says hello, you actually have to open your mouth and say hello back to that person."

She replied, "New Yorkers don't have time for that."

I eventually won her over. Although, she had to practice a lot. After that, we hit it off.

We communicated as if we'd known each other for years and that worked for me. Our first serious talk was about athletes and dating. She said, "You know, athletes have a reputation for chasing lots of girls, and I'm not having "none-of-that. I don't play cat and mouse games. If you have any thoughts of hooking up with different girls on campus, you best get it out of your head because I'm not the one to mess with. You will not disrespect me!" She continued, "I get your friendly personality (coming from the South) and your Southern charm. That's what I liked about you when we first met." She finished with, "And I won't stand in your way of football or try to change you."

"During my migration up I-95, I didn't dream of chasing a dorm full of co-eds. I didn't think of relationships as a game, and I had no thoughts of hooking up with different girls. The only people I planned to chase are quarterbacks and running backs in spring practice, and the only game on my mind is football. I had no thoughts of hooking up with as many co-eds as possible or even finding a girlfriend," I said. "My mind was racing as I traveled north to Cheyney, and the one thing I thought about was making the football team. I have one shot to get it done." I told her.

As our conversation continued, I could feel the emotion in her voice, and it was very familiar to me. Her voice reminded me of the loving tone I had heard growing up around so many strong Black women. I didn't feel my manhood was being tested or questioned. I appreciated how firm, direct, and straight up she was with me. She cared about me as a person and not as an athlete. She understood how important playing football was to me. She was going to support me all the way. She spoke from the heart, and I respected her more because of it. All I had to do was not blow it.

At eighteen, I was seriously dating someone for the first time and our relationship was built on communication. I quickly realized the woman I was dating from the "Boogie-Down-Bronx" had no problem speaking her mind and offering her opinion. One night she told me, "We were lucky to start our relationship without any issues." She said, "Think about it, we're single and no one back home is holding us back. We started the semester at the same time, and no one has tried to come between us, and I didn't need to compete for you." She added, "Girls like guys who stand out, especially athletes."

I asked her if she could handle dating an athlete. She replied, "Yes."

I often found myself discussing the female-to-male ratio with my co-ed classmates. I did notice more girls on campus. Some girls believed the lack of male options played a role in their dating frustrations, and most believed athletes had more dating options compared to the average guy on campus. I started to take notice of the relationships my teammates were in, as well as, a few athletes from the other sports. It was a small sample size on a small campus, but from what I could tell, more guys than not were in positive relationships. I was having a positive dating experience as a freshman athlete. And what did I know? I had no real dating experience to look back on. I was coming of age and dealing with a relationship on a higher level—a young adult level—and I was learning on the fly.

I didn't lose my focus because I was in a committed relationship. I had something to prove as a new freshman athlete, and my status was unclear on campus. I wasn't given or awarded anything. I had to earn it, I kept telling myself. What I didn't do was pull out my, *I'm an athlete* card or use the "I'm the best player on the team" line with the girls to improve my position or popularity on campus. A few of my soon-to-be teammates jockeyed for their places on campus and went hog wild because of the higher co-ed ratio. These guys acted as if they just unwrapped the best Christmas gifts of their lives. It was as if they had no experience being around so many beautiful Black women daily and as if they didn't know that Black women came in all shapes, sizes, and shades. These guys came from predominantly White high schools or from schools where the student body was equally White, other, and then Black.

Unlike a few of my teammates who didn't grow up in a predominately Black community, I was very familiar with my community's multiple realities and identities of Blackness, and it was no different at Cheyney. I understood why a few of my teammates and other athletes who didn't grow up with the full Black experience would be excited to see a variety of Black women on campus. And because of my background, I knew that not all Black women were carbon copies in personality or appearance. Our campus was graced with different shades of beauty, intelligence, and ambitious Black women—dark skin, brown skin, and light skin.

First was the dark-skinned beauty (referred to as "Queen"); next, the brown-skinned beauty (affectionately called "Black Butterfly"); and then the light-skinned beauty (described lovingly as "Redbone"). Overall, the girls enhanced the environment, culture, and traditions of Blackness on campus.

As an athlete, the social dating climate on Cheyney's campus was no different than what I noticed in my high school and Black community. I understood that choosing a light-skinned girlfriend meant my classmates would be assuming that that's the Black identity I felt more comfortable with, and I knew I would be opening myself up for conversations and criticism—for or against.

By the time I arrived on campus, the dating scene was playing itself out from the previous semester. The male athletes with good reputations were already dating, and there was nothing odd or surprising about their character regarding dating. Most of the athletes valued their personal relationships as much as their sports careers and academics. These athletes treated their girlfriends with respect, and their actions spoke volumes around campus. Their girlfriends were not only attractive; they were talented, assertive, and had style and smarts. I assumed the couples focused on their futures, personal goals, supporting each other, and maybe spending the rest of their lives together. Each couple managed to stay clear of the silly behavior happening around them, and they were all the better for it. I planned to do the same.

With my experience as an athlete that attended an all-Black high school and family members that attended HBCUs, I knew that when you're an athlete attending a Black institution, your stardust wouldn't be so big and bright. In the world of dating, I wasn't going to be the only big man on campus. I understood that athletes from Black schools shared and competed for the spotlight with the guys from other organizations: drum majors from the band, fraternity brothers, homecoming kings, and student class presidents. I knew that athletes at a Black school held no hierarchy of popularity over male students involved in other school activities. I understood that more than a few of my teammates who didn't have that previous experience.

For most of my classmates, falling in love was wonderful, and staying in love was hard. But for athletes, dating was complicated.

TOPIC 10. WINTER RACE

I clearly remember—and will never forget—my first winter up north. It was a shock to me. The snow started to pile up before I got to Cheyney, and it piled up even more during my first two months there. My Florida winter jacket wasn't thick enough, and my shoes weren't the type of footwear needed to walk on the frozen lake-like conditions. My hands and toes felt icy all the time, and my face was frozen into a permanent smile. I was now a refugee from the South and had to learn to survive in my new weather environment.

My girlfriend and I would take romantic walks around campus after it snowed. She was raised in this harsh winter, so our attitudes toward winter were opposites. During our walks, she would tease me by saying, "Toughen up, you're not in the South anymore." One night I was headed to her dorm after dinner, and I slipped on black ice. My feet flew into the air, but I was able to turn while I was airborne so that I wouldn't hit the back of my head. I had just learned the hard way: When the sun turns part of the snow into slush during the day, and the temperatures drop at night, the slush freezes.

I wasn't prepared to deal with the winter conditions, and I learned walking around in sneakers was not a smart or safe thing to do. I was always cold and miserable on the inside, but I didn't show it. Down south, we called the strong winds during our short winters, "The Hawk." The hawk up north was more like an eagle—bigger, stronger, and more powerful. The winter was dangerously cold and would cut through skin like a knife, but when it snowed, it was also beautiful in its own way.

During snowstorms, Mother Nature could be passive-aggressive. She'd create an incredible scene of beauty, a work of art, while potentially destroying that very same artistry with her swirling winds. The winter storms would fill me with anxiety as I stared out my dorm window. When a snowstorm was in full effect, it was altogether something different. Inches of snow looked like icebergs, and feet of snow looked like small mountains to me. I noticed my Black classmates from the North didn't feel the same way I did about the cold weather, nor did they react the way I did. My first winter up north was challenging to say the least. I had to learn how to have fun on the weekends in the dorm without finding trouble. Growing up in the South, where the weather was nice seventy to eighty percent of the time, it made it easy for a kid to stay entertained outside. I noticed my brothers and sisters, the students from the North, dealt with the snow differently than my brothers and sisters from the South. My classmates from the North seemed to not be bothered by the winter weather. Their attitude said, "It's no big deal," but for me, I acted as if I was in Antarctica or Alaska.

My winter's isolation on campus was unbearable, memorable, and beautiful all at the same time. Mother Nature added the unknowing to my tank of anxiety, like adding wood to a fireplace, as I waited for spring football practice to start. And at night, when the moon shined on the white wintery campus, I knew it would be an experience I would never forget.

I had to share the anticipation with someone. It was nice to cozy up with my girlfriend on those long winter nights. The snow blanketed the campus, and when the sun rose in the mornings or reappeared from behind the grey clouds to show off Mother Nature's artistry, I saw the sparkles in the snow as a reflection of the stars in Mother Nature's eyes. Winter's beauty can soften any man's heart, so I forgave Mother Nature for her passive-aggressive actions.

Although the winter was hard for me to deal with, I never felt out of place and as each day passed, I realized more and more that I could handle it. I didn't like it, but I could handle it. I didn't struggle academically because my freshman classes were the basic introductory classes. One of my classes was physical education. I signed up for it because I thought it would be an easy *A*, and I would be indoors. What I didn't know was that the teacher had a different plan. He desired to teach us something new, not the traditional sports kids in the Black community played, such as basketball.

So I decided to learn something different. I chose to learn how to play tennis. I didn't know any kids in my neighborhood who played or even liked tennis, but I wanted to give it a try. My teacher brought in an outside instructor for the lessons, a White female tennis coach. She talked to us with respect, showed patience, and gave us confidence, and my impression was that she genuinely cared about her students. After a few weeks of lessons, the tennis instructor gave every student she taught a tennis racquet to keep, and I planned to hold on to mine for life.

During those winter months at Cheyney, there could've been a lot of free time on my hands to party, but I didn't—no beer, no smoking weed, and no drugs at all. I only hung out with the guys a little bit to take a break from studying or from working out for spring football practice or if my girlfriend went home for the weekend. I didn't want to waste time or blow the opportunity I was given. I went to every class, even if it was snowing or if the temperature was dangerously cold. I was already a late entry into college, and I didn't want to fall further behind. I never made it to Philly during that first semester. If Carl or Reggie were headed to Philly, I would turn them down because I wasn't ready to venture out to the big city yet. I didn't have the extra cash to spend on things I didn't need.

By the time winter was approaching her passive-aggressive end, I was feeling like I had been on punishment. I looked forward to the spring weather and football practice on the field. I had participated in the team's winter off-season strength and conditioning workouts held in the gym. I had to shake the feeling of hibernation off that had nestled itself in my soul during the winter. So I started to prepare for spring practice on my own by jogging around the campus when the weather cooperated, and if I thought I wouldn't freeze my butt off. A few times as I took a run around the campus community, I noticed local families, and what I saw was that they were all White. The town of Cheyney was a White community.

TOPIC 11. ISOLATED RACE

As the spring weather approached, my confidence grew. I started to notice the neighborhood and town where the university was located. The local Cheyney community was nonexistent and every student knew it. We were isolated and separated from the world. There were no streetlights, no corner stores, no fast-food restaurants, and the public buses stopped running after a designated time. If you commuted to the Cheyney campus from Philly, you missed the bus leaving Cheyney, and you didn't have a friend on campus who would let you sleep over, you would be up the proverbial creek without a paddle.

I grew up in what most people would call an all-Black neighborhood or all-Black community. To say "majority Black" would be too vague since the percentage would vary from fifty-one to ninety percent. The first street I remember living on was Darlington Drive, and there were no White people on my street. As a matter of fact, there were no White people on my grandmother's street or in her neighborhood, and I don't think it would have mattered. As a kid growing up in an all-Black neighborhood, I didn't feel racism or discrimination on a daily basis. To feel it, I had to travel to a White community, the White side of town, or "to the other side of the river . . . not the other side of the train tracks, " as people would say. (There were a lot of train tracks in the Black community.) And there were no White people on the other side of those tracks. I needed to travel outside the Black community or to a White-owned business like a restaurant, hotel, car dealership, retail store, or an all-White community.

I had heard about racism and discrimination from the Black elders in the church, adult family members, neighbors, students, and teachers at school, coaches, TV programs, and the news. When I was nine, we moved to Cavalier Road, a few blocks from my future junior and senior high schools. I don't remember any welcoming committee or someone knocking at the door saying, "Welcome to the neighborhood." What I do remember was a White family living across the street and next to my godmother. From time to time, I saw them get in their car, drive off, and return home. They were nice, in terms of waving in hello. Sometimes I might get a word of *hello*, but more often than not, my family received a wave, and that's it. My mom taught us, "When they wave, throw your hands up, and wave back." In the South, if you were born and raised there, you understand what Southern hospitality is. The unwritten rule of Southern culture in my home was this: If you make eye contact with anyone—Black or White—you acknowledge them in some way. If a greeting is not extended or returned, someone is going to run into a big problem, or you would know where you personally stood with that person from jump-street.

My family or godmother never had a problem with the White family, and I hope they didn't have a problem with us. However, they weren't very sociable. We acknowledged their presence, and they acknowledged ours. I never stepped on their property, and they never came over to ours. During the holidays, if the White family had people over to visit, they stayed inside. I never saw them barbeque outside. It was like they lived on an island, isolated from everyone in the neighborhood. As a kid growing up in that type of environment, you understand or accept that's the way it was.

My family also lived six houses down the street from another White family, and they were senior citizens. I guess they, too, decided to stay instead of fly out of the neighborhood when Black families started moving in. I only saw them once in a blue moon. Honestly, I saw more snakes, alligators, and wildlife in my neighborhood than I saw of them. I would sometimes see someone peeking out of their window as the other kids and I from the block played football or raced each other in the street.

Each of those White families kept to themselves for the most part. Why did they isolate themselves from the rest of the neighborhood? The White families in my neighborhood were never attacked or asked to leave or get out. Rocks were never thrown through their windows, and they weren't called horrible names, such as the *C* or *H* words, nor were they called "PWT" or "the White devil" because that wasn't true. And their homes were never in jeopardy of being burned down. They were retired or working folks, just like the Black families in my neighborhood.

For the most part, Whites lived on their side of town or in their White communities and Blacks did the same. I had little contact with Whites growing up and what contact I had was while working a summer job, with one or two teachers, within the school system, or competing against majority White football teams. I had a few White teachers, but none had a positive impact on me. I actually had a White teacher tell me not to get my hopes up about going to college. You know the exercise where teachers ask the kids to tell them what they want to do after high school. My teacher pulled me to the side at the end of class to tell me to think about a trade school. Was my teacher a racist? I don't think so. This teacher was liked by the student body and had been a teacher at my high school for a while. This teacher had also taught my older sister, and my sister had done very well in her class. My teacher probably didn't see the potential or my dream; she couldn't feel my passion for playing football. With that White social experience behind me, I didn't let it get me down; rather, I let it fuel me. I used that experience to stay focused on working as hard as I could to graduate from high school and find a way to get to college and play football.

The campus was located in a rural farmland community with nothing to do but go cornfield hopping. That's it. You couldn't even go cow tipping because none were around. The Cheyney community was very quiet at night, and the closest store was miles away by foot. If you weren't from the area or familiar with the Cheyney community, it would have been a disappointing sight to see.

As a freshman, living in the Cheyney community didn't bother me. I was there to play football, but I could understand how the upperclassmen were frustrated, bored, or not interested in hanging around on the weekends. I was unfazed by the realities of the campus community because of my experience with the White families in my neighborhood. They were invisible or they wanted to be. I didn't notice if there were any White students or professors on Cheyney's Historically Black College campus, and I wouldn't have made a big deal out of it if there were. I didn't keep my head down or try to avoid any White students. I was focused on starting my college career on the right foot so I could play football. The fear of failure was always on my mind as a first-semester student.

Despite the isolation, Cheyney was like my second home. Cheyney's Historically Black campus became familiar to me. It had the Black experience I had heard about from my female family members. The parties, music, fraternities and sororities, sports, other activities—the good and the bad. A few of my high school classmates and friends in my neighborhood attended other HBCUs, like FAM-U, Spelman, Morehouse, Xavier, and Savannah State. I wondered how many HBCUs were located in the same type of community as Cheyney.

TOPIC 12. FLORIDA BOYS RACE

A small number of my teammates were Floridians, and they were the only group of guys I hung-out with. I had the feeling we loved football more than most of our teammates from other parts of the country. The Florida boys talked about the actions and techniques needed to win. I was excited to get on the football field with each guy in our group. Reggie and I represented northern Florida. My roommate Carl was from Liberty City, and the rest of our crew were from Hollywood, Belle Glade, Daytona Beach, and Pahokee. The Florida boys had fun in the dorm; it seemed like we all lived on the same floor, so it felt like we lived in a bubble. We were antsy for spring practice and itching for the spring weather to arrive. The parties on the floor were small events. They were basically small get-togethers—nothing to miss class over or get kicked out of school over or get in trouble with the head football coach and the university over.

College coaches began checking on their athletes in the '80s to make sure the athletes went to class because of the low graduation rates in the past. It was widely reported by the media that Black athletes, overall, were not graduating as frequently. I was afraid to miss or cut class, not because of the punishment by the coach, but because of my mom. I was afraid of what would happen to me if my mom found out. So hanging out all the time or missing a class was, to put it simply, not an option for me. One thing we did during the cold weather was play cards, specifically Spades. I could play but I didn't. I was concerned about getting caught up in something (gambling), which could turn out bad. Some played for money and others played for bragging rights, and that's the only way we played in Florida. It always got "real" serious and competitive quickly. I was pretty good because I had learned from watching and playing with my family members.

My uncles, Joe and Billy, were really good players, but the best player in my family was my Aunt Regina. I spent more time learning the game from my Uncle Joe, but my Aunt Regina was the queen at Spades. She was the best. Not only did she whip you, but she would also embarrass and destroy you. She would talk so much trash while kicking your butt that she would mentally and emotionally hurt you. She was so much smarter at the card game compared to anyone else in my family. As emotional and competitive as she was at playing cards, we always had a good time.

The girls on campus loved watching guys play cards. There was something about the Florida boys. We maintained a certain culture of carefreeness, craziness, toughness, and coolness that radiated from our group. And the girls liked it while the brothers from the North despised it. We had very pretty girlfriends, and the brothers from the northeast (mainly the Philly Tri-State area) weren't too happy about it. The brothers from the North teased the brothers from the South about how we talked. I noticed the brothers from the North spoke differently, as well. I assumed it was part of their Northern culture. The brothers from the North used words I hadn't heard before, like "youse," and most of them talked very fast.

Most of the fellas from Florida were Dallas Cowboys fans. Even the guys from central and South Florida were Cowboys fans, and I didn't understand why. The Miami Dolphins' home base was in South Florida, and the Miami Dolphins were winners. I remember, back when I was a little chocolate morsel watching TV at my grandmother's house after church, the teams everyone watched were the Dallas Cowboys or the Oakland Raiders. I had become a big fan of the Cowboys, and I loved seeing the Cowboy's cheerleaders. I wanted to play for the Cowboys, like most kids who were Cowboy fans do. The guys from the Philly Tri-State area hated the Cowboys and their fans. I did dislike (not hate) the Philadelphia Eagles, New York Giants, and the Washington team (which, as I write this book, is changing its name). I didn't like those teams because they competed against the Cowboys. However, I couldn't stand the Pittsburgh Steelers because they hurt me when they beat the Cowboys in one too many Super Bowls.

Finally, the start of spring practice had arrived, and I was more than ready for this football tradition. I had a few butterflies in my gut, but I kept reminding myself, *this is what I worked so hard for back home*. I didn't feel out of place in the locker room. I was in the right place, right where I wanted to be, and I knew it was where I was supposed to be. I was so pumped up I could have taken on two offensive players at the same time—a tight end and running back—in an Oklahoma drill. The coaches gave their normal motivational speeches. The current players got the chance to meet the new guys (walk-ons) trying out for the team, and the graduating seniors were able to say a few words to inspire the team. Each player received his practice jersey and equipment, selected a locker, and was handed the spring practice schedule and the date of the Blue & White scrimmage.

On my first day of spring practice (outdoors and in pads), it was cold, and a little snow remained on the field. Between classes during the day, I couldn't stop thinking about how cold it was. I knew I wouldn't be able to handle practice if I didn't do something. So I wore long sleeves with the bottom thermals, rather than the thin long johns that cowboys wore in the spaghetti westerns in the movies; I wore the thick ones contractors wore when they're outside working a hard labor job. One or two of my teammates from the North asked, "Why are you wearing long johns?"

I raised my voice and said, "I've never played football in this chilly weather."

I looked to the Florida boys to learn how to deal with how cold it was during practice. I was a year and a half removed from putting on all my football pads and a helmet. They gave me a little more confidence to go out and show everyone I could play. I was excited and nervous at the same time. I had to mentally prepare to block out the pain that was coming my way and focus on the pain a few of my teammates had coming their way. In order to get my mind in the right place, I listened to some music with the Florida boys.

TOPIC 13. APRIL 1ST RACE

The music in the Philadelphia area was unlike anything I had ever heard on the radio in my hometown. Philly had more Black radio stations compared to my hometown. They called it "urban radio." It was the way Philly radio grabbed me and forced me to lock my dial onto their stations. I was a new listener to the Philly sound, and I was a music transient from the South. I realized my love of music traveled well because music was in my blood. I had sung in my junior and senior high school concert choir. My mom loved to sing and had a great voice. My dad was a music teacher, musician, and he had performed professionally for a short time.

I remember the day the breaking news came across the Philly radio airwaves. It was a Sunday afternoon. I was listening to the R&B radio station in the Philly Tri-state area. The DJ, complete with a deep voice said, "Breaking news! Marvin Gaye is dead." I couldn't or didn't want to believe it was true. For a short time, some of my classmates believed it was an April Fool's joke, and if it was a joke, we all agreed it was a sick and despicable one. Some dismissed the news as rumor and wouldn't even talk about it.

When I looked outside my dorm room window, I could see the word had begun to spread from dorm to dorm, one floor to the next, and one room to the next as doors opened or closed. I could see and hear students racing through the halls, past my door, running up and down the stairs to get to a radio or TV. And one thing happened in unity—everyone turned up their volume.

As the DJ played Marvin Gaye's songs one by one, it was as if the entire campus was in church. He encouraged everyone to sing along and let our raw emotions, the passion and grief, ring from our voices. The DJ became the choir director, and we were his choir. I could hear who grew up singing in church by the way their voices carried throughout the halls. Even the casual fan of Marvin's music was pulled into the moment. That was Black culture at its best, and that's how the Black community paid homage to Marvin Gaye.

I got through the death of Marvin Gaye by the grace of the DJ. I don't remember who the "jock" was, but I remember the feeling of comfort and closure he transmitted through the airways, and it was soothing to my soul. I never heard anything like it. The DJ gave his listeners, me included, the chance to mourn together. His impact was therapeutic. He took me through the range of emotions that I'm sure everyone was feeling. There were so many questions the DJ helped me answer by living in the moment to celebrate Marvin's life and music. I was enticed to think deeper and go beyond the music to find its meaning.

My mom had a few of Marvin Gaye's albums. My first time seeing him on TV was on "Soul Train" on Saturday afternoons. But the greatest memory I had of Marvin was him singing of the national anthem at the 1983 NBA All-Star Game. Marvin became my favorite singer of all time that day. Whenever my girlfriend and I were having struggles in love, like most couples, I knew enough to play some of Marvin Gaye's music to help heal the situation. Marvin was able to deliver a message with his voice and words that most men could only wish they had the skill to recite.

Marvin Gaye had been the Black community's musical, cultural, and socially conscious leader. His music during the difficult times of race relations and times of war was the healing message Americans needed. Marvin's lyrics of love were simple to understand, made sense, and forced every American who listened to look in the mirror. There's no debate in the Black community that Marvin was "the man" of his era.

That day, for hours and hours, all I heard were Marvin Gaye songs. I didn't think anything of it because music and singing had always been one of the ways the Black community paid their respects to our heroes and leaders. Music was the great equalizer . . . and had been for Black Americans from the church to the streets and everywhere between.

I couldn't afford a boom box at this time, so the music I had came from a standard clock radio with a nice volume meter. And what's ironic about that day, as college students, my classmates and I had musical freedom. There were no parents in our dorms telling us to turn down the music! We had full control of the dorms and that was no normal day. I had the feeling that April 1st would never be the same again.

TOPIC 14. WOLFPACK RACE

Monday's practice started out somber and slow. The locker room conversation was centered on the death of Marvin Gaye, but eventually, my teammates and I moved on to the reason we were all there—to play football. Spring practice was scheduled for a few weeks leading up to the big scrimmage, and I felt the pressure. I wanted to represent the Cheyney University Wolfpack and wear the blue and white uniform in the fall, so I put a lot more pressure on myself. I admitted to myself that the pressure was on me to practice well and to get the attention of my position coach.

The pressure I felt in high school to be recruited and earn a college scholarship was a different type of pressure than the pressure I felt at Cheyney. The pressure in high school stemmed from the desire to be noticed by a college recruiter or scout and earn a scholarship. The pressure as a walk-on in college was to get noticed by both the head coach and your position coach to earn a spot on the team. I was eager to walk on the field and make some noise by showing what I could do. I was jacked up to hit someone hard. There's a crazy feeling most football players get (more defensive players than offensive players) when they make contact with another player. I loved that feeling, the joy of knocking the snot out of another player. And yes, it hurt most of the time, but most, if not all, players learn to block it out. That's what separated the men from the boys.

I was very excited to be on the field with Reggie and even more excited to talk about it after practice. Knowing he had my back and I had his was the type of teamwork, chemistry, and player relationship most athletes look for and try to reach in our country's ultimate team sport. Every day during warm-ups I gained more confidence. I was able to look my potential teammates in the eyes and see if they had what it took to compete or if they were chicken. I looked to see if they had the toughness I knew I had and knew I was able to dish out every day. After a few hitting drills, done every day at the start of practice to get warmed up, I knew I was able to compete on the Division II level. Without a doubt, my confidence grew and my odds of making the team increased every day. I just knew I could be a walk-on player and make the team.

The team wasn't stacked with an overwhelming number of top talents, blue-chippers, all- state, or high school gridiron greats, but they were good and hardworking teammates. A few of my defensive teammates had accolades they bragged about. A couple of them had played for a high school state championship, and they had the rings and varsity jackets to show for it. I wasn't sure if any of my teammates were a legacy athlete, meaning their dad, uncle, or a family member played for Cheyney in the past.

I hadn't been in a locker room in a while, and that took some getting used to because of the "boys will be boys" behaviors and conversations that took place there. The school's mascot came to practice one day and walked up and down the sideline. A few of my teammates talked about tackling the mascot during practice, and that's when I knew I was in the football culture again.

One thing I noticed during an intense locker room conversation was that a few of the guys were talking about what football program where they almost landed. You know, the shoulda, coulda, or woulda conversation. Where they should have, could have, or would have gone to college to play, were it not for . . . and the excuses or half-truths came. My two thoughts were, "What's wrong with these guys? Aren't they happy here?" Unlike a few of my teammates, I was not unhappy. I was excited, but I didn't have any other options. All I needed to do was get my body back in football-playing shape, and to do that, I needed to work hard and let loose by dropping someone every day in practice.

After every practice, my body was sore and physically drained. But all I could think about was the physical pain I had felt during my workouts back home and the sadness of not living my dream of playing college football and those recent memories got me through. My hard work back home began to pay off. My position coach told us (the secondary/ defensive backs) that we were shaping up and coming together. At the start of spring practice, there were questions that needed to be answered. Who would fill the spots of the graduating seniors? I knew Reggie and Carl (my roommate) would likely fill those spots because they were ahead of me with experience and time on the team.

I had to set my sights on making the team first; then I could reach for the stars in the fall preseason training camp. I improved every day in practice, laying the foundation to make the team. I played well enough in the spring Blue and White scrimmage to make it on the depth chart, and I looked forward to working out with Reggie in the summer to prepare for preseason practice. I wasn't looking to just suit up. I wanted to play—and make plays—for the Wolfpack.

Cheyney was a Division II football program that competed against West Chester, Lincoln, and Bloomsburg Universities, to name a few. The football team had put together a 3–7 record in the previous season, but it didn't matter to me. By the time spring practice ended, my confidence was strong, my college experience was shaping up well, and I'd settled into my second home away from home.

TOPIC 15. HAPPY RACE

I had spring fever. I had overcome the challenge of making it through my first winter and college spring practices. I had accomplished my goal of establishing myself as a player in the Blue and White spring game. I was on my way to playing college football in the fall. I had a beautiful girlfriend, and my grades were good. Everything was great.

I began my Easter weekend prepared to do nothing but hang in my room, listen to music, and call home to talk to my family. I couldn't go home to Florida just for a weekend; it was close to the end of the semester, and I was low of funds. The campus was quiet, peaceful, the quad was empty, and the whole place felt like a ghost town. I think ninety percent of my classmates went home or some other place for the weekend.

My girlfriend headed home for the break to spend some time with her mother. She caught the bus from campus to Philadelphia to take the Amtrak train to New York. After she got on the bus, I walked back to my dorm. I ran into one of my classmates, Tracy, sitting in the lobby. Tracy was from Pittsburgh and asked me what my plans were for the weekend.

"Nothing."

He told me about a party off campus and asked if I wanted to hang out.

"Yeah, why not?" I figured this was my chance to get off campus and explore outside the Cheyney community. I hadn't ventured off campus during the entire semester, other than jogging around the neighborhood.

Tracy's high school classmate attended a university nearby and was on his way to pick up whoever wanted to come. The plan was to meet at the front desk around 7:00 p.m. Tracy's high school classmate arrived, and his name was Happy Dobbs. My first impression of this guy was good. He had a big smile—as if he was, in fact, happy all the time—and a friendly personality. He asked me if I had plans for the next day.

"No."

"Go pack an overnight bag and pack some hoops clothes," he told me.

I figured we would be playing hoops on Saturday, as most athletes did when down time was at our feet. My roommate wasn't around, so I couldn't tell him were I was going, and I couldn't find Reggie to tell him either. We loaded into the car and headed to the party.

We had a great conversation on the way to the party. I learned that Happy played basketball at Villanova University. He was a senior point guard standing six feet, four inches tall. I had never heard of Villanova, but I didn't want him to know that. Happy asked me a few questions about where I was from, what position I played, and why I had come so far north to play football. I answered his questions, explaining my love of football and how Cheyney was my only option.

Happy asked, "Do you think you'll make the Cheyney football team?"

I told him that I had a good spring practice, and I had made it on the depth chart for the fall season.

I answered the rest of his questions with confidence. Happy told me he had played in my hometown in December (four months back). Villanova had played Jacksonville University (JU) and lost and then played Auburn and lost. It was at that moment that I remembered the night after working out in front of my house that I had watched the late local sports news highlights of the Auburn basketball team—the team with the player I had referred to as "the big boned-country brother from off the farm—" badly beating a team with a Wildcat as their mascot. I said to Happy, "That was you guys?"

He grinned and said, "Yes!" I asked Happy what the player's name was who had dunked all over his team. He replied, "Charles Barkley."

Happy's team hadn't played well the entire tournament. "Will some of your teammates be at this party?" I inquired. He was sure a few would be. I asked him about his school's football team. Happy told me about Villanova's football program, how it had a long history, how the university had dropped the football program a few years ago, and it was now bringing the football program back in the fall. I said, "That's good news! No one wants to go to a school without a football team."

As we made our way to Villanova, Happy mentioned a few of the former Villanova athletes (Howie Long, Sydney Maree, and Rory Sparrow). I recognized the name Howie Long. He was playing for the Oakland Raiders at the time. I acted as if I knew the other athletes and the history of its sports program, but I didn't have a clue. You can chalk it up to youthful and regional ignorance. Happy was co-captain of the team and had a good chance of getting drafted to the NBA. That's the reason we were playing hoops the next day. Happy was working out to prepare for his possible future in the NBA. I had a good feeling about him. He had a genuine big smile, but I knew his first name wasn't really "Happy." It had to be a nickname, and it was easy to see why that name had stuck. I decided to ask him about his birth name a little later.

It seemed like a long ride to the party because I hadn't been off campus at all, but in reality, it was only a twenty- or thirty-minute drive. I tried to check out the scenery as we drove, but we were traveling in the pitch black of night. We reached Villanova's campus, and the first thing I saw was the beautiful church. It was facing the main road, and the floodlights that shone on the church were very bright so that all the people who drove by could see its beauty.

I said to Happy, "You have a church on campus?"

He replied, "Sure," as if this was a normal thing.

I thought, "We don't have a church on our campus."

Happy pointed out the basketball gym and the turf football field, but I couldn't see it clearly. I had only seen a turf football field on TV, and I hoped to see it up close before we headed back to Cheyney.

We pulled up to a building somewhere on campus and got out of the car. I asked, "Who's having the party?"

He replied, "It's a BCS party."

"A who?"

He said, "The Black Culture Society; it's a cultural and social organization on campus."

I thought, "I've never heard of that group on our campus, but I guess I'm about to find out." When I walked into the party, I assumed there would only be Black students, and I was right. I couldn't put my finger on the finite reasons, but the atmosphere was different at this place, and I liked it.

Happy introduced me to a few of his teammates and a few basketball players from other local schools who had been invited to the party. He also introduced me to a few of the beautiful Black ladies at the party. I remember one of the girls who caught my eye. She was, without a doubt, gorgeous and classy. Happy told me that her father worked at the university and was a school legend. Everyone seemed happy and excited to be there. The conversation was on a different level than anything I had experienced, everyone representing themselves with class. Later, Happy asked me if I was having a good time.

"Yes, the music is jumpin' and the vibe is nice."

At the end of the night, we headed to a dorm to call it a night, and when we arrived inside, I couldn't believe how big it was. Tracy and I had our own rooms during the visit. The next morning, Happy and Tracy came to get me for breakfast. I was prepared to walk to a different building for breakfast, but we walked downstairs and stayed inside the dorm. "A cafeteria in the dorm?" I thought.

Happy said that after breakfast, we'd be headed downstairs to the gym to shoot some hoops. In my mind, based on what I had seen so far, I couldn't even begin to picture it. "I can't wait to see this."

TOPIC 16. RECRUITED RACE

After breakfast, we hung out in the cafeteria, just talking with other guys. On the way to the gym, we passed the indoor swimming pool. Tracy and I looked at each other with disbelief. Tracey said, "Get the heck outta here!" and I said, "A swimming pool, a basketball court, and a cafeteria in the same dorm!" I yelled out, "This place is the bomb!" I'd never seen or heard of anything like this type of dorm, and I was impressed. As I walked into the gym, I was a little nervous, but the anxiety quickly dissipated once I got on the court. After a few minutes of shooting around and warming up, I was introduced to a White guy, Teddy Aceto, Jr.

The gym was packed with Black guys and a few White guys looking to get a run in. The atmosphere inside the gym reminded me of back home at the park, times when the basketball court was heavy with ballplayers, which meant the games were going to be competitive and rough. Everyone wants to win so they can stay on the court, but the only difference for me was, I had never played with a White dude, either on the same team or even on the same court. There were certainly no White guys on the court back home in my park. I wasn't intimidated because my confidence was higher compared to when I was back home. I told myself to be the athlete I trained to be. I got picked to play on the same team with Teddy Jr. and soon discovered that White dude could play. There was no doubt in my mind that Teddy was a better player than me; in fact, he was one of the best players on the court. We played well together. I was impressed by Teddy's athletic skills and his intense personality on the court. Teddy wasn't afraid to be on the court with so many Black athletes and neighborhood ballers. He more than held his own. He even embarrassed a few of the brothers that played D-I ball. He continued to impress me.

After playing for a long time and then watching a few games, we headed back upstairs to grab a shower and have lunch. Teddy ate lunch with us, and I got to know him a little better. He asked me, "Do you want to meet my father after lunch?"

I said, "Sure why not?" I can honestly say, I had never met anyone like Teddy.

After lunch, I went to meet Teddy's father. Happy drove us to the sports gym called the "Field House." The gym was located on the corner of the main street traffic and the entrance to campus. I thought, "What a great place for a gym." Happy had pointed out the Field House the night before. Now, I could clearly see the gym and the football stadium.

Before I reached the gym's door, it hit me! The experience felt like I was being recruited, and it felt good. I didn't say anything because I didn't want to embarrass myself by asking and being completely wrong. Even though I had never been officially recruited, it felt that way because my high school coaches talked about it, and a few of my teammates had talked about their experiences while being recruited. We walked into the Athletic Department offices, and I was introduced to Teddy's dad. For some reason, at that moment, I remembered what my mother had always told me: "When you meet and talk to a White man for the first time, look him in the eye, and make sure he can hear you." And I did just that.

"Hi, Mr. Aceto. My name is Bo-Dean."

He extended his hand, and I extended mine. Mr. Aceto welcomed me to the university. Happy and Teddy told him I was a football player at Cheyney. Mr. Aceto informed me of the history of Villanova football and the status of the football program returning as a D-I AA program. I learned why the university had dropped football for three years. (There had been no scandals or issues with the NCAA.) There were a few football players who had stayed after the program was dropped, and he hoped I'd get the chance to meet them in the fall. Mr. Aceto talked about how college football was evolving and getting better on every level, and the university and alumni were in a position to move forward with a new program. And, of course, the students were ready to get football back on campus.

He asked me all the standard questions, such as where I was from, where I had played high school football, who my coach had been, and how my grades were at Cheyney." We continued our conversation, and I had the feeling everything was going well. Then he asked me, "What do you think of the Villanova campus . . . are you having a good time?" He also asked if I had any questions. I told him I had never been on a campus like this, I enjoyed the BCS party, and I was having a great time.

Mr. Aceto let me know that a head coach would be hired soon, and we finished our conversation with a few things for me to do when I returned home for the summer. Then he gave me his contact information. When I look at his business card his actual title was Dr. Aceto. And from that moment on I knew how to address him. Dr. Aceto asked Happy to show me the turf field and the coach's offices. Happy walked Tracy and me down to the astroturf, and I finally got the chance to walk on a turf field for the first time. It looked like grass, but it didn't feel like grass. I started to imagine playing on this field. As we walked off the field and crossed the track, Happy told me more about the young lady I had met at the BCS party. He told me her father had been a track star for the university, "way back in the day."

"What was her last name again?"

He said, "Collymore."

I walked out of that stadium thinking, "What a great place to play a game."

After checking out the stadium, we headed back to Cheyney. Happy wanted to get Tracy and me back before we missed dinner. The Villanova community was like nothing I had ever seen. The campus was much bigger than Cheyney's campus, and the community felt like a small city. I had no idea if the Villanova community was a White community, like Cheyney's, or a Black one. I'd heard of upper class, well-to-do, Black private schools up north, and I knew Cheyney wasn't one of them.

As far as I could tell, I had seen more Black students and very few Whites during my visit. Happy and Tracy caught up on things happening in their hometown during our drive back. I sat in the back seat, thinking about the great experience I had just had—meeting all those people at the BCS party, the large dorm experience, playing hoops, eating breakfast, and that darn swimming pool. But the best part was meeting the AD and his son.

Happy got us back to Cheyney in time for dinner, and I finally asked him what his first name was. He smiled and told me, "Frank." Happy asked, "Did you have a good time? Did you like 'Nova?" I told him I had a great time, I loved the campus, and everybody was cool. Happy felt I would be a perfect fit, and that I should think about transferring to Villanova. We shook hands, and I thanked him for a great time and for introducing me to the AD. My feeling of being recruited was confirmed, but I wasn't being recruited by a coach. I was being recruited by the Athletic Director, his son, and the co-leader of the men's basketball team.

My unofficial visit to Villanova wasn't the traditional way of being recruited, but to me, it felt like the stars had all aligned. Villanova hadn't named their head coach yet, but they were close to selecting one, and that didn't scare me. I wasn't worried because the AD told me they needed players, everyone would be starting from scratch, and there would be scholarship opportunities for the players who made the team. My decision to transfer was going to be the toughest decision in my life, and that decision would test my relationships and friendships I had made during my freshman year at Cheyney. Also, I wondered how my family and friends, the ones who had created the opportunity for me to attend Cheyney, would react.

TOPIC 17. LEAVING MY RACE

I couldn't get my visit to Villanova off my mind. I wanted to enjoy the last days of the semester like the rest of my classmates, but I couldn't. I wanted to hang out in the Quad like my teammates and classmates, but I didn't. I had gone through the coldest winter of my life, and the spring-like weather I was used to from Florida had finally arrived, and I couldn't enjoy it. I had two things on my mind: telling my girlfriend about my trip to Villanova and then telling her about the possibility of me leaving Cheyney.

One day after class, we went for a walk around campus. The weather was perfect, and the campus was beautiful. But before I told her about my trip and my plans to leave, I thought, "I can't let her influence me. I have to be mentally tough and stay on course."

I dove in.

After I told her about my visit, that's when the conversation really began. She hadn't heard of Villanova either, and she wanted to know what was so special about it. I told her that I didn't know much, other than what I noticed on my visit. I didn't have to remind her of how much I wanted to compete on a higher football level and how competitive I was. I told her it would be a big step up to D-I. We ended our conversation with me stressing that Villanova and Cheyney weren't far from each other, and it wouldn't be a long-distance relationship.

I remember the day I decided to transfer and leave Cheyney. I ran into a senior and former player, Andre Waters, before the end of the semester. I only knew Andre as part of the Florida boys' crew and what Reggie and other teammates told me about his play on the field at Cheyney. Andre attended our spring practices from time to time and that's where he saw me making a name for myself, on the practice field. Andre was born in Belle Glades, Florida and attended Pahokee High. He was a starting cornerback and a three-time PSAC All-Conference player. I knew Andre as a kind, funny, approachable, sometimes quiet, and all-around nice guy.

I told him about my visit to Villanova, and I asked him what he thought I should do. At that moment, I was nervous to hear what he would say. But he told me to go for it because he "believed I could handle it." He said, "There was something about me," and he felt I would be okay. Andre gave me the push I needed to give it a shot and make my decision—at least in my mind. My heart wasn't quite on board, but it would soon follow I was going to transfer to Villanova. Andre told me to take a chance . . . that's what he had done. Andre had given it a shot and chased his dream of playing pro-football by trying out for the Philadelphia Eagles. Andre was undrafted when he tried out for the Eagles. I gained more respect for him because of his courage.

As the oldest HBCU in America, Cheyney had its issues, but I was clueless about any of them because I was happy to be in college, and I was on my way to officially being a member of the football team. I loved everything about Cheyney, including the dorm experience and campus grounds, however the sports facilities were similar to my high school's facilities. Though, that didn't matter to me. I didn't judge or complain because Cheyney was a small school. I made it through my first semester, and I was never in jeopardy of being placed on academic probation. As I told people who asked me about my classes, study habits, and grades, "I can't get bad grades, my mom will kill me."

I had a positive experience at Cheyney University, but I lived in a bubble—a cocoon—and the world was much larger than the campus and the local community. I discovered there was more out in the world for me to learn, places to develop, and reasons to grow. The campus felt isolated from the rest of the world. I grew up in an all-Black environment, a much larger Black environment, compared to the campus life at Cheyney University.

The campus was quiet on the weekends because most of the students from the Tri-state area went home. I gained so much confidence during my time at Cheyney in my personal relationships, educational experiences, and throughout the spring football practice. I was confident I would get the chance to become a starter on the football team in the fall, but I guess in the back of my mind, I was still competing with myself or looking for that bigger challenge and the opportunity to play football on a higher level. I was pretty sure I had found it in Villanova, which provided that bigger dream that I had developed as a kid.

I was excited about the possibility to play football at Villanova and during my last few nights at Cheyney, I thought about it over and over again. I felt bad and maybe a little confused about leaving Cheyney for Villanova, but I was going to follow my gut. I had no idea how I was going to tell Reggie about my weekend at Villanova and that I was leaving. My decision to leave Cheyney wasn't because I was unhappy with the university. Cheyney's storied history was second to none. Since 1837, Cheyney educated born-free Africans in the North, runaway slaves, and freed slaves from the South. When Cheyney was founded, their mission was to educate "Colored Youth." More importantly, it was known for aggressively educating, training, and developing Black students, who would go on and grow up to become leaders in the Black community and in the United States. Cheyney was a symbol of Black Power.

Cheyney's location was special, a beautiful scenic drive out to the rural farmlands outside of Philadelphia. The school was separated from all the other schools in Philadelphia of its age. I didn't see it when I arrived in the dark of night but during the day, I could see it clearly. I didn't need to be a Tuskegee or Harvard graduate, nor did it take a rocket scientist to figure out why. I'm sure the born-free Africans or freed slaves during Cheyney's growth and development didn't care where the campus was located or how far it was from the city of Philadelphia.

The Black community had its first Black educational institution to call its own. Cheyney educated the Black masses during slavery, reconstruction, disasters, wars, economic depression, the industrial revolution, Jim Crow, and the Civil Rights movement. The campus was far enough from the city so the students enrolled could focus on their educational goals—earn an undergraduate degree and a post-graduate degree, prepare for a life after college, and achieve the most important goal, the Black American dream. Cheyney's Historically Black campus played a very important role in Black history, in the Black community, and in the United States. Cheyney gave me the jump-start I craved and the confidence I needed to take advantage of the opportunity that fell into my lap to transfer to Villanova. I will never forget Cheyney for as long as I live.

TOPIC 18. JACKSONVILLE RACE

My time at Cheyney had come to an end. My first college semester was over. I had completed the second most important race of my life by earning a spot on the football team, but that part was just beginning in the fall. I had the feeling of joy and pride because of what I had accomplished. My nightmare, disappointment, and the pressure I felt after high school graduation was gone, and my dream to play D-I college football was coming to fruition. And yet, it was a bittersweet time in my life. I finally told Reggie about my weekend visit to Villanova and my plans to transfer to Villanova, if I was accepted. I could tell he was disappointed. I was unsure how my decision to transfer would affect our relationship, but I was willing to face it head-on. I figured we would talk about a week or two after returning home. As my mom would say when facing tough decisions, "Give it some time, sweetie," and I did.

Reggie and I rented a car to head home. As we traveled back to Jacksonville for the summer, I became excited because I was headed back to my roots. My mind was racing, and my heart was about to pop out of my chest, again. I had so much to think about. I walked through everything I missed from my neighborhood. I couldn't wait to see my mom and the smile on her face when I walked in the door and to talk about my college experiences with her, my godmother, and my sisters. San was about to graduate from high school. And when I wanted the chance to visit my baby sister, Alicia, and her siblings, all I had to do was walk around the corner to their house to see them. I looked forward to the smell of freshly cut grass, the smell that rained in the air after waking up on Saturday mornings to cut the grass in our front and back yards and my godmother's front yard if it needed it. I was excited to catch up with my best friend, Jesse-Duke, if I could find him. San had stayed in touch with his family while I was gone. I was sure I would run into other high school teammates over the summer. And that meant catching up on what they were doing and what I've been up to for the past five months.

I was jonesing for some Southern soul food. Something I discovered at Cheyney—not every Black person or Black family enjoyed Southern soul food, such as boiled peanuts, pig's feet, collard greens with oxtails or ham hocks, chitlins, boiled crabs (not steamed), grits with cheese, and fried pickles. Eating my mom's and grandmother's home cooking was at the top of my list. However, I knew in order to get some of my grandmother's delicious food, she had to see me in church on Sundays. I also looked forward to going back to J.C. Penny to ask about a summer job. And the most important thing I looked forward to was sleeping in my own bed. I realized I loved my hometown. I began to appreciate my hometown more and more. I laughed about it because I didn't dislike my hometown, but I had felt limited and stuck.

No matter how uneventful or unsuccessful the memories I had of my past in Jacksonville, home was home. My uneventful social life (all work and no play), and the unsuccessful athletic memories didn't matter anymore. I had my own college and football stories to share with my best friend, high school teammates, classmates, or whoever would listen. I could have the college locker room talk with my high school teammates; I could share with classmates the story of a college professor that reminded me of a high school teacher. I could talk about the campus cafeteria food and the difference between northeastern food and Southern food. And I could add some intel regarding the regional, cultural, and musical differences between Black folks in the North and the South.

I arrived in Jacksonville early in the evening. My mom was at work when Reggie dropped me off, while my sisters were home finishing up dinner. It felt good to see them again. San's dog, Chico, gave my arrival away by barking uncontrollably when I walked in the door, and my sisters yelled out "he's home" with excitement. Dinner was waiting for me in the stove. Fried pork chops with mac and cheese. I waited for my mom to get home before I ate dinner because I thought it would be a nice surprise to eat with her. My mom walked in the door about twenty minutes after I did, and it was an emotional moment when she saw me waiting at the kitchen table. I'll never forget it. I didn't speak to anyone outside of the family unit that first night; we just spent a few hours together. My mom was happy I had made it home in time for San's graduation.

I anxiously waited on the paperwork from the Villanova athletic director. I was filled with a ton of emotions—excitement, nervousness, and a little sadness about my plan to transfer. I waited to bring up my opportunity and feelings of transferring until after San graduated from high school, because I didn't want to rain on her parade, and I didn't want to jinx my opportunity.

One week after San's graduation, I couldn't hold it in anymore. One day, everyone was home and it was quiet in the house. We gathered around the kitchen table, and I told them about my plans. The mood changed as if lightning had just hit the big tree in our front yard—electricity. And the look on everyone's face said it all. My mom had the "I don't know what you mean look." San's look said, "Let's get this over with, I have places to go and things to do," and even San's dog looked at me like I was a two-headed squirrel. Her dog had never liked me.

But Pam's reaction was all too familiar—the look that screamed, "I'm going to hurt you." She immediately slipped into her very serious voice, direct, firm, and slow, which meant she was not at all happy. I described the events that had led up to my decision, and I believed that Villanova was a Black school. San said, somewhat Black or all Black? Pam told me I was wrong, and that I had lost my mind. She told me that Villanova was a (PWI) Predominantly White Institution. A private, elite, and very expensive school. I replied, "No it's not!" I was naïve and too stubborn to believe her. I didn't believe her because of what I had seen and experienced during my visit.

During our family's big pow-wow, Pam looked at me and said, "Just because Georgetown has all Black basketball players on its team doesn't make it a Black school." And before I could ask if Georgetown was an all-Black school, San looked at me and shrugged her shoulders to mean she had no help to offer me (I was on my own). I could see the conversation wasn't going my way, so I called Pam the name PJ (short for Pamela Joyce) a few times, and she replied. "Don't call me PJ to soften me up." And before I could say what was on my mind, Pam stormed out the front door and walked across the street to my godmother's house. In a few seconds, she and my godmother were headed back to our house, expressing the full, Black woman, firm, and direct walk. I could see my sister talking to my godmother, explaining the situation, and it didn't look good for me, at all.

My godmother was not only our neighbor but also our academic and financial aid advisor. She was the person my mom leaned on for advice regarding her kids' education. It started with Pam, and now she was being called on to advise me. Juanita earned her undergraduate degree from Spelman College and her master's from the University of North Florida, spending her entire professional career in higher education. Juanita's calm presence helped the situation. She told me that if I transferred, it's possible the credits I earned wouldn't transfer, and I would be starting over. I was okay with that. She wasn't there to change my mind, but she was there to provide me with all her wisdom and experience. I knew Juanita would support whatever decision I made.

As we continued discussing my potential transfer to Villanova (I say potential because I was ninety percent sure I was going to transfer if I got accepted), I learned the difference between Cheyney and Villanova was night and day, or Black and White, from Pam and Juanita. It was a tough conversation to have with Pam because of her efforts to get me into Cheyney, and I didn't want her to feel like I had betrayed her and her efforts. After the conversation ended, I went outside and hung out in our backyard on my brother's basketball court to think about every point each person made during our family meeting.

I didn't know if Pam was trying to steer me away from the PWI because I had no experience in that environment or if she wanted me to play football and graduate from Cheyney. After shooting hoops for a while, I thought, "This is going to be my decision because, for most of my life, I have done what others want me to do and not what I want to do." It was time to put my foot down. I remember thinking that I didn't want to be that guy—the one who talked about what he could've, should've, and would've done if the opportunity to play for another football program came his way. I reminded myself after my visit to Villanova that there's more of the world to see. And that's one reason why I had seriously considered transferring. Either way, it was going to be my decision.

TOPIC 19. TRANSFER RACE

Two days after announcing my big news, my Villanova application arrived. I noticed it on the coffee table after returning home from working out. I tried to play it cool by leaving it on the dinner table for Pam and my mom to see. However, I made sure to be nearby when Pam noticed it. I didn't want it to walk away and end up lost.

Pam surprised me by offering to help me fill it out, but I wanted to complete as much of it as I could on my own. I eventually walked across the street to my godmother's house and asked her to help me complete the application. She was happy to help. Before we started, she wanted to know if I was ready for my new environment. I reminded her of my experience at the FCA summer sports camp I had attended a few years back. I had no problems and had enjoyed a good time.

After I completed the application, I showed my mom and told her I was going to mail it back. She said, "I don't know much about what you're doing, but I trust you, and all I want for you is to be happy." Now it was time for me to step up my game because I was about to get the chance to step up and play D-I football. And if my sister and family members were right, I needed to start saving money and operating on a shoestring budget. I had no time to bum around the house. I had to manage my time and get back into my workout mode. I had so much to do and so little time.

One day, not long after this, my grandmother called me. She expected to see me in church on Sunday with my sisters. I said, "Yes, ma'am. I'll be there." I was so consumed with the second religion in the South that I had almost forgotten that my grandmother would be looking for me in church when I returned home. I knew one reason my grandmother wanted me in church. She wanted to keep me grounded and not let me get a big head. And I knew she looked forward to when the preacher recognized and introduced all the college students who returned home for the summer to the congregation. I remember Aunt

Rosylin, Pam, and many young members of the church being recognized in the past. I looked forward to teasing my grandmother for not smiling when it was my turn to be recognized, but that Sunday she surprised me. When I was introduced, she smiled, and quickly pointed for me to sit down. That was her way of not showing up the other church members. I was the only male that day in church to stand and be recognized.

The day it happened, the day my acceptance letter arrived, it was my birthday. I had just finished mowing the grass and had started cleaning the outside utility closet. I heard our mailbox open and close. I went to grab the mail and place it in the house. I noticed the mailman was White as I watched him deliver the mail next door. I had never noticed him before or seen a White mailman deliver mail to my house before. I knew White mailmen existed but not in my neighborhood. I was surprised because the only White people I saw were the White family that lived across the street, and that was only a few times per week.

As I gathered the mail inside, I noticed a larger-than-normal white envelope with blue ink lettering. It was addressed to me, and I quickly raised my eyes to read the name of the sender. Villanova University. I sat down and then stood up at the kitchen table. I was nervous. I retrieved a knife from the drawer and opened it. I had to read it a few times before I believed what I was reading.

I had been accepted. If I had all of my football equipment on, I would have run through the side door of our house. Thank God I didn't. The only person home with me was San, so I ran to the back of the house toward her room. I should have knocked but I didn't. I yelled, "I was accepted. I am in!" I handed her my letter with no idea what to do next. I ran back to the front of the house—for what, I didn't know. I could hear San scream with joy as she read my acceptance letter. I had to tell someone else, but there was no one else to tell. My mom was at work and Pam was out with her friends.

A couple hours later, Pam pulled into the driveway as I was finishing cleaning up. I hesitated to tell her at that moment because I didn't know how she would react, but she could tell something was up by the look on my face. So I said, "Villanova accepted me. I'm in." And again, she surprised to me with her reaction; she was happy for me. She wanted me to call Mom at work. I didn't. I wanted to wait for her to come home to share the news while everyone was home.

My mom returned home from work after an agonizing wait, and it was a great family moment, but my mom was concerned about my new environment based on Pam's description about the university. So she made me promise to listen to my sister about what I was getting into. Before it got too late, I ran across the street to Juanita's house to give her the great news. She was happy and excited for me, and I asked her to help me with my first semester financial aid package. She agreed.

Later that night, I called my girlfriend to share my good news about Villanova. She wished me happy birthday and congratulated me on my acceptance. I was truthful with her about the conversation I had with my family. I told her I could be wrong about the race demographics of the university.

"I'm not one hundred percent sure the Black students I saw at the party reflected the true population of the student body."

She wanted to know what I was going to do. I had made my decision, and I was going to follow through. I, again, referred back to my experience at the FCA sports camp I had attended back in high school. She didn't think I should compare my high school summer camp experience to what I could face on the college level. I assured her I would be fine and that I wasn't the only Black athlete to attend a White school. I said, "Besides, Pam could be wrong; the ratio could be fifty, fifty." But she was still concerned our relationship would suffer because we wouldn't be on the same campus. I reminded her that I wasn't transferring out of the state, and Villanova was only about twenty miles away. I wanted her to feel comfortable about my decision, but that didn't help. I couldn't make her feel any certain way. We agreed to continue the conversation later.

I was still on cloud nine and jacked up about getting accepted, and I needed to burn some energy. I did the only thing I could do at that time of night. I went out to my street and ran wind sprints. As I worked out, I pictured myself playing on the Villanova turf; I saw myself playing either free safety or strong safety, defending half the field or making a big time hit on a running back or stopping a tight end from catching a pass. I worked out until I couldn't run any further. I had lost track of time, and I noticed that every house on my street was dark. It was time to call it a night.

I woke up the next morning to go for a long run and work out at my former high school. I started my run in the direction of my high school, but soon after, decided to turn around and go in the opposite direction. I went in the other direction because I had experienced a life-threatening event at the local corner store. I was jumped and had a gun pointed in my face. It's not easy to forget having to look down the barrel of a gun. I saw my life flash before my eyes, as the saying goes. That corner store was the bane of my existence.

The longer I ran, the more my mind cleared. I didn't notice how far I'd run, but then I recognized the neighborhood I was in. I decided to stop by my high school teammate, Jason Pearson's, home. Jason was a three-year starter at the tight end position. We played side by side on offense for two years. San mentioned to me, the day after I left for Cheyney, that Jason had stopped by to see me. So it was a perfect time to return the favor, stop by, catch up, and talk football with a guy who loved football as much as I did.

Jason was known in high school and in the neighborhood as "JP." It was good to see him and his family (his mom and sister, Stacey) again. We talked for a little while, and then I wanted to continue my workout. Jason decided to join me.

After our run, we headed to the high school to work out for hours. He invited me back to his house for lunch and then to the park for a few games of hoops. By the end of the day, we had renewed our high school friendship. I told him about my plans to transfer to Villanova, and he was excited for me. He joked with me about my moving up to Villanova and D-I football was like the TV show, "The Jefferson's." Yeah, JP was right—I was moving on up.

In a few weeks, I would be leaving for Philadelphia. JP was my sounding board. He listened to the concerns my sister had about me transferring. We had a few conversations about the guilt I felt about leaving Cheyney. He reminded me to remember the words our coaches had drilled in our heads: "Sometimes you got to move on and focus on the next play."

During my remaining weeks in Jacksonville, I'd hang at his house and he at mine. We'd reminisce about games we won and lost and the most important game against our high school archrival, W. M. Raines. JP stopped over a few times to pick me up to go to parties, and my mom would let him know (in her serious voice) he was to make sure her son didn't find any trouble out there. He'd reply, "Yes, ma'am." On my days off from work, we'd workout. He pushed me because he wanted me to be ready. The day before I left for Villanova, JP stopped by to give me a pep talk. His friendship meant a great deal to me. We developed a special bond because of our experience playing football together, side by side.

CHAPTER IV

Villanova Race

TOPIC 20. TRAIN RACE

I t was a hot and humid day. I didn't know where the Amtrak stop was nor had I ever ridden on a train before. The train station's parking lot wasn't a big one. It was like the train stations I had grown up seeing on TV in the spaghetti westerns. I could tell my mom was tired of working a few extra hours. I wanted her to drop me off, head home, and get some rest, but she wanted to stay until I boarded the train.

We talked while waiting for the train to arrive. It was eerily similar to the talk my sister gave me eight months earlier but also vastly different. She asked if I was ready.

"Yes. Remember, Mom; you taught me not to do anything half-way," I said.

But she really got my attention with her reply, "When you get on the train, sit wherever you want to, and don't let anybody tell you to move or tell you what to do."

I said, "Don't worry, Mom, I'll be fine." I noticed she was more intense this time compared to when I left home for Cheyney. Maybe it was because I had traveled with two guys from the neighborhood she knew. This time, I was traveling on my own and to an environment I knew nothing about. Once again, my mom had to watch me leave, but this time I was off to another world. She seemed uncomfortable, uneasy, and more concerned than excited for me. The only thing I could think of was that maybe she had a bad experience traveling on a train. She never told me about any bad experiences in her past, but I did know she had traveled to Detroit when she was younger.

Our history of race relations in the South had been well documented. I remember when I was a kid, my mom was looking forward to getting a promotion at her job. On that day, when she walked in the door after work, my sisters asked her if she received the promotion.

She simply said, "No." The look on her face said it all. But the next words out of her mouth were, "Maybe next time." So my sisters decided to bake a cake, and we never heard anything more or talked about it ever again.

Growing up in the '70s, I saw things on the TV news and heard a lot of stories about discrimination on the radio and in church from families, friends, and the Black community. However, my mom wasn't the type to blame all White people for everything negative that happened in her life or to other Black people in general.

I could hear the train coming down the tracks. It was time to leave. I gave my mom a big hug and kiss, and we said our good-byes. I grabbed my belongings and walked to the train platform. To lighten the mood and reassure her, I turned and said, "Don't worry, Mom. I'm going to play D-I football, and I'm going to make that team." As I boarded the Amtrak train to Philadelphia, I was hit with several emotions. It was another of those bittersweet moments filled with excitement, anticipation, and the unknown. However, I had more confidence in my skills and faith in my heart. And I knew I was going to bust my butt to make the team.

I remained excited and focused during the train ride of my life to Philadelphia. I was on Amtrak, and this train ride was my horseshoe to a better football opportunity. I was nineteen years old and feeling good about myself. I was prepared for my seventeen-hour (or more) ride to Philadelphia. I didn't have the option of taking a plane because we couldn't afford it. Nonetheless, I was ready to begin my journey. I picked a place to sit and put my stuff away. I had a storage trunk and two shoulder bags.

I was mentally prepared to enjoy the long ride through all the small towns and cities with names I did and didn't know, all over again. I was hoping to see different details this time around from my train ride, ones I didn't see during my previous car ride. I was looking forward to each stop because this ride would be different from my first migration up north. I wondered how many people were headed to the same destination, Philadelphia, as me. After I settled in my seat, I looked around while the other passengers picked out their seats and prepared for their trip. I'm sure a few passengers noticed or sensed that it was my first train ride. A few of the passengers said hello and a few made eye contact, and we exchanged smiles. It was good to acknowledge a greeting when offered one.

It was a different type of greeting and exchange. I was the only Black person in my train car. I didn't get on the train searching for a racist or racism, but I was prepared for it. Nor, did I get on the train focused on looking for other people that looked like me; however, I did find myself waiting to see that second Black person boarding the train. My mom always preached, "Be aware of your surroundings." It was drilled in my head and probably drilled in every Black kid's head by parents while growing up in the South. But for me, I was curious about where the other passengers were going—back home, to work, to see family, on vacation? Was anyone, like me, headed to college?

Hours into my ride, my mind was still racing to Philadelphia. Finally, I started to simmer down from all the excitement and the emotions of saying goodbye to my family. I started looking around the train, up at the ceiling, at the door when it opened and closed, and at the people who entered and exited the boxcar through those doors. I looked out the window at the trees, the clouds, the sky, and then my eyes caught a plane in the air. I thought maybe my trip back home would be on a plane. I had taken a bus trip to football camp back in high school and the bus ride was nothing like this train ride. The locomotive was massive. It felt a little like the beginning of a roller coaster ride, and while on the way up, a little jerk here and a rock there vibrated beneath me. I don't like roller coasters because I fail to appreciate that feeling I get on the way up . . . and definitely on the way down. That train was a tub-like bullet machine racing its way from one stop to the next. I continued to feel a few eyes checking me out and my instincts kicked in every time. I could hear my mom's voice between my ears: "Don't attract attention." So I played it cool. My boxcar never reached full capacity, and every now and then, after a stop, some people would get on and a few would get off. And I was still the only Black person on the train.

Now the train was moving faster and headed into North Carolina. Again, I was traveling through the former Southern Confederate states of Georgia, South Carolina, and into North Carolina, and I didn't have any problems regarding my race during the trip. I noticed some of the people were sitting around me and near me, but no one sat in the seat in front or behind me. I didn't feel unwelcome, out of place, or as if I didn't belong. My focus was to enjoy the ride, get to Philadelphia, find my way to Villanova, and play college football. During my long ride, as new passengers boarded the train, I had short conversations with a few, and there were times during the conversation when the awkward silent moment happened. It wasn't a bad feeling, but I wasn't familiar with that feeling, so I pushed through that part of the conversation by smiling.

When the darkness of night reached the train, I became tired, and thought, "What if my sister was right about the ethnic ratio of the university? How I would fit in?" I didn't travel all the way to Cheyney because everyone on campus was Black. And I wasn't going to go or *not* go to Villanova because everyone could be White. I was going because I wanted to play football at a higher level; that was my dream. I was hours away from reaching my destination. I wondered if I was lucky to be the only Black person to travel on the train without any problems, or was I just the only Black person headed up north on this train. I didn't know. I was counting down the time until I reached Philadelphia.

I finally arrived in Philadelphia at 30th Street Station, but I hadn't reached my final destination. I followed other passengers off the train and up the stairs into the main concourse. It was unbelievable. I looked around and up toward the ceiling, the way most first-time travelers do when they arrive at a new destination. I'd seen the station on TV, in a movie, but I couldn't remember what movie. What a massive and beautiful building! I couldn't believe how huge the train station was. People were everywhere. They were walking fast (that pace was familiar to me), sporting serious looks on their faces. I could smell coffee in the air, but the odor from the food was unfamiliar to me. The station was loud. I could barely hear myself think. I heard a clicking noise, so I looked in that direction, and there it was, a huge scheduling board, with all the incoming and outgoing trains. I walked outside to check out the view. There were taxis and people everywhere. A street preacher caught my eye—that was a first for me. I was in the heart of the big city, and all I could think was, "I never got to see this at Cheyney."

I walked back inside to find my way to Villanova. I asked a Black woman passing by how to get to Villanova, and she pointed to the ticket window. I asked the person behind the window. She hit me with a question: by train or trolley? I didn't know the difference. I must have had a look on my face, the one that told her I didn't understand because the attendant gave me a look in return . . . the one that said she assumed I was from another planet.

"What's the difference?"

"How much do you want to pay?"

One way would get me there directly, and the other, I needed to jump off the train and catch the high-speed line at 69th St. I responded with, "The closest transportation to the football stadium." And I paid. I was given a transfer ticket to get me there. Then, I was on my way. I thought, "I just got off a seventeen-hour-plus train ride to Philadelphia and what? I gotta take another crazy train to Villanova? I'm done with trains after this."

I made my way to each train stop while carrying my heavy bags and made it on the high-speed line to the football stadium. I stood in the front of the train to make sure I didn't miss my stop.

I finally arrived at Villanova. The Black train conductor asked me if I was a ballplayer, and I replied, "Yes!" with enthusiasm. Then, he wished me "good luck" in a weird way (I thought), as I walked off the train.

21. OVERCROWDED RACE

I stood on the Villanova train platform to take in the view. Everything was moving fast, and the campus seemed bigger than I remembered. The parking lot, gym, stadium, and entrance to campus were in my view. I made my way to the football office, and the first person I ran into was a White guy. He was sitting in a red Porsche convertible in the parking lot. I sent a hello his way, and he replied, "Yo, bro, how youse doin'?"

I thought, "What did he just say?"

His name was Tony, and he seemed okay but there was something familiar about him. He was wearing a white T-shirt, smoking a cigarette, blasting his music, and sported a thick gold chain around his neck. He wanted to know if I was a ballplayer.

"Yes, football."

He meant basketball. He reacted as if he didn't know Villanova had a football team, and then he seemed to have remembered the football program was starting up again. He offered to give me a ride to the football office. I took him up on it. During the short ride to the office, I had to do a double-take as I noticed a large number of White students at the traffic light, but I could barely hear myself think because the music in his car was so loud. We made it to the office, and I thanked him. He left me with, "Yo, if you need anything let me know. I'll see you around campus, bro."

That was the first time a White dude called me "bro," and I didn't know how to take it. I had a feeling, from that moment on, there were going to be a lot of "firsts" for me at Villanova. I took a deep breath and walked in the football office.

I checked in with the football office, and none of the coaches were there. The office assistant, Ms. Bangs, helped me out by confirming all the items on my checklist and pointed me in the right direction for registration, housing, meal plans, orientation information, and more. As I walked out of the football office, it finally hit me what was familiar about Tony. He talked like the boxer, Rocky Balboa, from the movie *Rocky*. I thought maybe Rocky was his hero.

As I walked across campus to the registration building, I didn't see one Black person at all. There were White folks, probably students, for as far as my eyes could see, and I looked everywhere. I didn't recognize the place I had visited in the spring, and it was much bigger than I remembered. I pictured my sister's face and heard her voice: "Hardheaded . . . I bet you'll listen to me next time." I was, without a doubt, in an environment I'd never seen or been in before. But I was okay. I was there to fulfill my dream. I did notice more eyes on me compared to my first full day at Cheyney. However, I still felt the same excitement and was ready to play some football.

I made it to the registration office and waited in the line for a while to get my room assignment. I looked around the entire time I was in line, and I still didn't see a Black person. When I finally made it to the front of the line, there was a problem. I had no designated housing. I didn't lose my cool, snap, or assume someone was out to get me. The woman assisted me immediately. She went into scrambling mode, and I heard someone in the background mention the lottery system, referring to student housing on campus. I had no idea what that meant. She apologized many times.

I noticed everyone in the office was nice to all the students. I gave them as much information as I knew. I was told there were no open dorm rooms due to overcrowding. I was asked if I could commute until a permanent room assignment opened, and I said, "No, ma'am. I'm from Florida, and I'm here to play football." The look on her face said it all. I had never seen a White person turn a little red-faced before. A few calls were made to the football office, Athletic Department, and the Student Life office. I was advised to go see Father Stack in the Student Life office. When I walked into his office, I almost called him Pastor Stack, but I caught myself. Fr. Stack and I had a brief conversation, and he made a call. I headed back to the registration office, and I eventually received a temporary room assignment and a key.

I was on my way to Griffin Hall, and the map directions pictured my dorm across the street from the church, the same one I had assumed was a Baptist church on my first visit. As I approached the church, I stopped in front to take a good look at the crosses on top. The church was massive, and the style was amazing. I wasn't sure what kind of stone the builders had used to construct it, but I'd never seen anything like it in my neighborhood. I had seen churches like it on TV, in the old vampire and Frankenstein movies. My eyes had more than each could see. I imagined three of my grandmother's churches fitting inside the campus church.

Then, I raced to my temporary room, quickly unpacking my things, just in case they decided to change their minds. I made it to my dorm, opened my room door, and my roommate was already there and unpacked. And he was White. I extended my hand, and he did the same. We introduced ourselves, and his name was Brian Shane, a.k.a. "Shane Bo." I thought, "What were the chances my first White roommate and I would share part of the same nickname!"

I liked the name Shane because it reminded me of the Western movie, *Shane*. We were about the same size, height, athletic build—he looked like an athlete. I wasn't in shock with having a White roommate, but I was confused about how I could have gotten it all wrong and my sister was right. I continued to think nothing was the way it seemed on my first visit.

I didn't know much about where I was or what to expect, but there was no turning back at that point. Shane Bo and I talked for a while, and he told me his dad worked in the Athletics Department; he was the assistant baseball coach. We talked about why we were sleeping in temporary housing and the timeline for getting our permanent dorm assignment. I learned the university was hard to get into and more transfer students and freshmen had shown up than they had anticipated. Shane Bo told me his dad expected it would happen because football was back. I told him that's why I transferred, to play football. Shane Bo didn't assume I was there to play sports. He was happy for me and wished me luck. He asked me if I had been recruited. I told him not by any coaches. I guessed what his next question would be, and I knew I would come off as naïve, so I decided to hold back the embarrassing part of my story. I shared the part about meeting "Happy" Dobbs, my visit, with Dr. Ted Aceto Sr. and Teddy Jr., and the rest was history. Shane Bo told me that Happy was drafted by the 76ers over the summer. I was happy to hear the news.

We spent about an hour talking and learning about each other. Shane Bo knew his way around the campus and offered to give me the first unofficial freshman orientation tour. We walked to Campus Corner Pizza and made our way for the center of campus, to the Connelly Center, to check out the scene and grab something to eat. A few minutes after we sat to eat, "Happy" walked in. I was *happy* to see him. The three of us talked for a little bit. Before we parted ways, I pulled Happy to the side and told him that I thought Villanova was a Black school. He smiled and assured me I'd be okay with everything.

I continued to hang out with Shane Bo for a while as we walked around the campus. We passed through the quad and went to the Field House to see if his dad was in his office (he wasn't). We stopped at Stanford Hall, next to the train stop, and headed back to our place by cutting through the parking lot. Because of all the walking and checking out the campus, I forgot to call my family and girlfriend. I called home to let my mom know I had made it safe, sound, and in one piece. I didn't talk long because it was a collect call, and I didn't want my phone call to be very expensive. I decided to call my girlfriend first thing in the morning.

I thanked Shane Bo for showing me around and then it was time to call it a night. He was out like a light. I lay in my bed, thinking about my day and all the things I had on my plate for the next day—orientation, check-in with the coaching staff, and hopefully running into more Black classmates.

I had a busy schedule, busier than I did at Cheyney. I finally received my permanent housing assignment, and I couldn't believe it. It could've been luck, or coincidence, or a helping hand. I was assigned to St. Mary's dorm. The same dorm I stayed in during my visit. As I made my way to the dorm, I prepared myself to meet a new roommate. Maybe he'll be Black, but I had been realizing over the past twenty-four hours that the chances were, he'd be White. I opened the door to a room with one bed. I couldn't believe it. I had a single—my own room—with a small, personal sink. My room was across from the men's room and shower room. And I thought, "I'll take it," but part of me also thought, "Somebody made a mistake."

Things were looking good for me, and it got even better. I learned we had a room-cleaning service. That's another thing Happy forgot to tell me. I moved in and continued to think about football and tried to put aside my thoughts about how many Blacks were on campus.

It took me a little time to get used to the fact that I had my own room. I decided to make it feel like my own. I did a little shopping in Philly. I wanted to make my dorm room feel like my home away from home. I picked up a few posters to hang on my wall, but the biggest thing I got was a Black Panther stuffed animal. As a kid, the only two comic books I ever read were one *Thor* and one *Black Panther* comic. I hoped if any of my White classmates came into my room, they wouldn't get the wrong idea about the Black Panther stuffed animal, but if they did, I would be more than happy to explain why I had it.

TOPIC 22. RETREAD RACE

After a few days of attending freshman orientation, I had started to think I was the only Black freshman on campus. I knew more Black students would show up for the official start of school, but I had no idea when I would run into them. One night after working my way through the tasks a new kid on campus must do, I finally noticed and met a Black classmate. I was on my way to the bookstore to purchase a few books, and he was leaving the bookstore with a Villanova T-shirt in hand. Buzz Bass was his name. He was an upperclassman.

I assumed Buzz was his nickname. We talked for a while and he invited me to his room to meet one of my soon-to-be teammates and more Black students. We talked sports on the way to his dorm room. He had been a running back in high school. Buzz was from Norristown, PA, and his major was engineering.

Along the way, we ran into the first Black female student I'd seen on campus. Buzz knew her, and he told me she was the personal assistant to Turquoise Erving, the wife of "Dr. J," Julius Erving. I didn't make a big fuss about it because I didn't want to come off as if I was only interested in who she worked for, so I played it cool. We talked for a few minutes, and I learned we had class in the same building. The conversation ended with, "See you around."

I made it to Buzz's room, and he introduced me to Nate "Skate" Bouknight, Jr., also from Norristown. I exchanged handshakes with Nate and his handshake was a little stronger than mine, and that got my attention. Nate was a transfer from Liberty Baptist College, and he was a defensive back, like me. I was pumped up, because not only had I met another Black student, but now, I had a friend and teammate to talk sports with and someone with shared life experiences. I had a feeling we would get along and I was right. We clicked right away.

I hung out in Buzz's room for a long time because his room was evidently "the spot" and more Black students stopped by—Adrian Farris, the only Black player on the baseball team and "EZ" Ed Pinckney, and Gary "Gizmo" McLain, who were upperclassmen and members of the basketball team. They were excited that football was back and planned to root for us all day, every day. Nate new everyone that stopped by the room. Nate owned a car, and he gave me a ride back to my dorm later that night. We talked about getting on the field and doing our best to make the team. He offered to help me adjust to my new environment because of his experience growing up in the area. I leaned on him to educate me on the Main Line experience, local communities, ethnic differences, and the Catholic culture at Villanova. Nate traveled around with a serious or intense look on his face, but once you got to know him, he was a really cool dude. He had a great smile and possessed a welcoming heart. Our mentality on the field was the same, to destroy every offensive player on the field. Nate identified himself as a strong safety, so I decided to try out for the free safety position. On the field, Nate wanted to blow everybody up (seek and destroy) all the time, and I had to be a little more patient as a free safety. Our personalities off the field were different. Nate was outgoing, and I was more laid back, likely because I was getting used to my new environment.

A large number of students and faculty were excited about the return of football, but I quickly realized that basketball was the second religion on Villanova's campus. I learned this after two weeks of talking to anyone that would talk to me. A number of my classmates were interested in my background, but I was a little hesitant to open up and share my entire life story. If someone asked if I had a sweetheart back home, I answered "no" and didn't go into the details.

My girlfriend and I decided to go our separate ways after she returned to Cheyney. My mind was clear, and I was able to focus on my new environment. The more I talked to my classmates, the more I learned. I remembered the story about the three upperclassmen still around (on campus) eagerly waiting for football to restart. I looked forward to our first players' meeting to see how many players transferred in and how many were "current students," hoping to walk on. I attended the first football meeting with Nate. We were surprised at the small number of Black players who were there trying out. It didn't take two hands to count five Black players (one on offense and four on defense) out of seventy-five or more in the room.

The head coach opened the meeting with a speech, and then he introduced all the assistant coaches. There were eleven coaches and only one was Black, Coach Brian Jones. All the coaches were relatively young, but there was one older coach; he was the previous head coach at Villanova, Lou Ferry. I could tell he was an old-school coach because he was chewing tobacco, and I knew I would like him. When the head coach introduced the defensive back coach, Paul Ferraro, that's when Nate and I looked at each other. Nate gave me a wink and a nod, and I smiled. The head coach, Andrew Tally, introduced the three players I had previously heard about who had committed to Villanova before the university dropped the football program. I hung on every word spoken by Todd Piatnik, Pete Giombetti, and Roger Turner. Each guy talked about how excited they were to put on a jersey again, the love they never lost for football, and the sacrifices they had made to remain at Villanova. I could relate with all three of them because of my experience wanting and waiting to play football again. Todd, Pete, and Roger were like Coach Ferry—the originals, the real deals, the blue bloods—and the rest of us were retreads from one football program or the next, and each of us had something to prove.

The meeting then shifted to providing the information regarding the program, process, and preseason activities. We were handed our strength and conditioning schedules and other information. Every player was expected to be in his best physical shape for our official "on the field practice" and in pads. We were separated into individual groups. Each position coach called out the player interested in trying out for a specific position.

Nate and I followed our position coach to the area in the locker room for our meeting. I stood with Nate as the meeting started, and I counted one additional Black player in the room. Three out of twenty—that was it. My attention turned to the coach as he reintroduced himself to the players. Coach Ferraro was from New Jersey and had been a defensive back in college. He coached at several schools before taking the job at Villanova. He had a bit of an edge to him. After the meeting, I told Nate, "I've never been coached by a White coach."

"Don't worry. Everything will be fine."

TOPIC 23. COACHING RACE

Both my mom and my grandmother taught me to listen to my elders—adults and teachers—and treat them with respect. I looked at my coaches as teachers. My high school coaches were Black men and my coaches at Cheyney were Black men. My high school coaches told me I was coachable, but I had never been coached, on any level, by a White coach, at least until I arrived at Villanova.

Coach Ferraro was an intense person. I thought he was more than likely born that way, and everyone on defense thought he had a screw loose. His communication style was to scream at the top of his lungs, and when we were in our meeting rooms, he spoke as if he meant every word that "microphoned" out of his mouth. I didn't have a problem with being yelled at, but I'd never been yelled at by a White coach . . . or any White man. I was raised by and grew up with Black women; they were the leaders in my family, and they could dress you down with a few words, yelling or not. I had encountered a few Black "ramrod" coaches that yelled, but Coach Ferraro was like nothing I had ever experienced before.

In the beginning, it was difficult to deal with "his in your face" intensity. Because I was from the South, if or when a White man got in your face, it was go-time. I heard my White teammates refer to him as a player's coach and not a coach with a fake or a "salesman" personality. So I decided to give him a chance because Nate felt that way, too. His coaching style wasn't going to stop me from living my dream. I was going to suck it up as best I could. When I made mistakes, he yelled at me, just as my Black high school coaches did.

One day at the end of practice, he pulled me aside and explained what he expected. He treated me with respect and showed me he cared, but I didn't know if I could trust him. I was looking for straight talk, no BS. As the days went by, Coach Ferraro, preached to his players, "be there for each other," and I remembered my high school coaches doing the same. But I could feel he meant it, and he wanted us to believe it and feel it in our bones and souls, too. He didn't seem confused about me or act as if I was a complicated Black athlete to understand or to get to know. His actions showed he deeply cared about my wellbeing.

And while Coach Ferraro was giving everything to our coach and player relationship, I had to adjust my feelings and thinking regarding being coached by a White coach for the first time in my life. I had to stop thinking Coach Ferraro was standing in my way. I had to evolve, so I did. I didn't offer up or use any excuses. I focused on listening and adjusting to his coaching style. He took the time to get to know me, not just where I was from, but also what made me tick. He wanted to know my goals and how I planned to achieve them. I told him I wanted to make the team and play football for Villanova. His plan was to drive me to be the best athlete I could be, and if I followed his plan, I would accomplish my goals. Sometimes, I felt he yelled louder at me compared to Nate or my White teammates. So I'd remember our one-on-one conversations at the end of practice, and that helped me stay levelheaded. I began to understand where he was coming from, and our conversations gave me the confidence to continue to work harder to improve.

I had no consistent Black male role models or mentors growing up to help me develop and stay on course in terms of my athletic potential. A few of my Black high school coaches (The Gaffney brothers) had filled some of that void until I graduated from high school, but after high school, it was all on me. I wasn't going to let what I didn't have stop me. I began to question myself and couldn't put my finger on what I was doing wrong or why I wasn't perfect. I knew I was a late bloomer, but I was getting frustrated. He pulled me aside and instead of yelling, he asked me to spend more time studying the playbook, not to solely rely on my athletic ability. His support fueled me to focus on getting the play call right. No one was named starter at the safety position, but day after day I earned more reps than the other guys.

One day after practice, Coach Ferraro shared with me that he thought I was a very good athlete and that I could play on this level. Hours after our conversation, I was stuck on his words . . . that he thought I was a good athlete. I had worked hard for a long time to move past the athlete with potential to be recognized as a good athlete. And at that point, I felt my hard work had finally paid off. Now it was time to spend more time studying the playbook.

As we got closer to the Blue and White scrimmage for homecoming weekend, I started feeling like everything was coming together. And then it happened. Coach Ferraro surprised me again. On my way to the practice field, he pulled me aside and asked me to help the upperclassmen pull the defensive group together. At that point in my life, I had never had a Black coach, Black man, or White man ask me to help lead a group, and it took me by surprise because our three upperclassmen were White and the honorary captains of the team. The fact that my coach thought of me as a leader in some way was good to know.

TOPIC 24. HOMECOMING RACE

It was two weeks before the big scrimmage and homecoming weekend when I bumped into my classmate, Mrs. Erving's assistant. We talked about Cheyney and why I transferred. She was familiar with the homecoming events held at HBCUs. She warned me to not get my hopes up about the on-campus events leading up to homecoming at Villanova. I took the opportunity and asked her about working for the Ervings. "Do you want to meet them?" she asked.

"Sure! If you're okay with it."

A few nights later, she took me over. I had no expectations about what might happen. I was excited, but I didn't get carried away or act like most out-of-control fans. I had a Southern, laid-back personality, and I planned to play it cool. The Erving family didn't live far from my dorm, about a mile or two. Although I was playing it cool, my heart was beating a mile a minute. All I could think about was what my uncles would say when they found out I met Dr. J. It's not every day you get the chance to meet a highly-public figure and living legend. At least where I came from, it didn't happen much.

We pulled in the Erving's driveway, and I gazed at all the cars in the driveway. It was a castle of a home, equal to about five houses put together on my block and boasted a huge backyard. It was much larger than the temporary dorm I had lived in. As a matter of fact, it was larger than some of the small dorms or office halls on campus.

I entered the house and the Erving family was in the kitchen hanging out and talking. I extended my hand to greet Mrs. and Mr. Erving, and his hands consumed mine. I gave him my firm handshake, as always. He introduced himself as Julius, and I didn't fumble my words.

"It's nice to meet you, Mr. Erving."

He replied, "Nice handshake."

And from that moment on, I never called Mr. Erving by his first name or by his worldly nickname (Dr. J). It wouldn't have been right.

Besides, that wasn't the Southern way to address grown folks. I couldn't believe it. I was actually in the home of Mr. Erving. He wasn't just famous; he was a living legend. I had images stuck in my mind of him dunking on Bill Walton of the Portland Trail Blazers and Magic Johnson and Michael Cooper of the Lakers. His highlights were like a stream of artwork, sculptured in my memory. Mrs. Erving showed interest in our upcoming homecoming weekend by stating that she planned to steer clear from the school's traffic that weekend.

The week leading up to the big homecoming game was electric. The campus was buzzing with excitement and renewed school spirit, but there were a few naysayers that only supported the basketball program. New faces were popping up on campus every day. I was in the locker room a few hours before practice, studying for a test. A media crew walked in, and I was interviewed about our reinstated program and the upcoming weekend game. My picture made it in the paper. I clipped it and mailed it home to my mom (with my signature). I spoke to San, my Irish twin, and she asked me about the homecoming events. I told her that from what I had gathered, Villanova's homecoming would be nothing like an HBCU's homecoming . . . or even our high school homecoming.

Later that night, I read in the paper that my old roommate Carl, from Cheyney, had been selected for the PSAC All-Conference List. I was looking for any homecoming information about Cheyney, reminiscing about the choices that had led me to where I sat. I continued the homecoming conversation with a White classmate from down the hall. He wanted to know what a homecoming was like at a Black school. I explained it the only way I could. "It's a combination of a Miss Universe contest, fashion show, royal wedding, music concert, barbeque, and family reunion. The students and universities start to prepare for the big event on the first day of school of the previous semester. The hype and history generate attention from the students, staff, alumni, family and friends, the local community, and the news media. And the main attraction is the marching band that performs the hottest music at half time." I finished with, "Villanova's homecoming and an HBCU's homecoming isn't on the radar for football players because we don't get to enjoy all the events of the week or the main event of the weekend, such as the half time show. We're too busy preparing for the game during the week and during the game, we're in the locker room at half time, probably getting yelled at." I smiled.

Each day, I learned something new about the history of the Villanova football program. The word on campus was that the team underachieved, didn't win enough games, had embarrassing losses, struggled to pack the stadium with students, and more people tailgated rather than attended the games. In the end, the Board of Trustees chose to drop the program. After the program was dropped, a group was created to work toward bringing football back, and the leader of that group was a former player and the director of the Wildcat Club, Bob Capone. I remember the day I met Mr. Capone on campus. He walked up to me, introduced himself, and had said he'd heard good things about me. I was blown away. Supposedly, this guy raised millions to get the program back.

The day of the game, it started out like every previous Saturday. Nate stopped by to pick me up, and he did most of the talking. Sometimes I had to tell Nate to simmer down on a few mornings while we headed to practice because he was so intense. But I didn't say a word that day. The stakes were high, and I had elevated my focus that morning. Nate later admitted, "It was like pulling teeth to get you to talk."

We arrive at the stadium and walked into the locker room. We weren't the first in or the last in. The music was coming from everywhere—speakers in the ceiling and some guys had their own boom boxes. I'll never forget Franky Baltimore, a running back from Harrisburg and the only Black player on offense. That guy was something else. He was always singing, and he talked a lot of trash. I'd never met a Black guy with his personality. There must have been something in the water around Harrisburg. I hoped he would be on the opposite team because I wanted to put a hurting on him to have bragging rights. No one knew what color jersey they would be representing leading up to game day. I looked in my locker and found my blue jersey. Nate held up his white jersey. So we'd be on opposite teams, and that was okay with me. As Nate put it, "You know it wouldn't be fair to have us on the same team." I got dressed and hung out at my locker to prepare for the game.

Coach Ferraro walked into the locker room and called out to the defensive secondary group. We gathered in the back meeting room. His pregame speech was short and sweet. No time to live in the past. Time to create a legacy of our own and have fun out there. He pulled me aside and hit me with a few things: "Be prepared to return punts if needed; make sure everybody talks to each other out there, and be patient."

My wait was over. For everyone associated with the university and those who loved football, the wait was over for them, too. It was time to play the game. I had lived through starting from scratch before, at Cheyney, and it was similar but different at the same time. During pregame warm-ups, I noticed how excited the three seniors were, the nervous energy pouring out of their bodies. I didn't hear anything for a few minutes or notice the crowd. I was focused on what I came to Villanova to do, earn a spot on the team. I could see Nate across the field, and we made eye contact a few times. We both came out hitting. It was like we had both flipped a switch. And when Nate made a big hit, I could hear the "oohs" and "aahs" and clap from the crowd.

The competition on the field was much higher compared to the competition at Cheyney. Our punter, George Winslow, was an NFL prospect. He reminded me of the Oakland Raiders punter, Ray Guy. Catching one of his punts was like catching a rocket on its way down, and that was the last time I returned punts in a game. Eventually, I looked to the crowd to see how much support we had. The stadium was full, and the crowd seemed to be having fun. The guys on the basketball team were there, showing their support. And I was happy to see, what seemed like, every Black student on campus there supporting the program. It was a great day. I played well during the game, but one thing I learned: I knew my coach yelled when I made a mistake, but I learned he yelled even louder if I made a good play.

That day, I earned a spot as the starting free safety on Villanova's football team for the spring, and it felt good. My dream had come true, and I felt like I had found a home.

TOPIC 25. CHAMPIONSHIP RACE

Football was reborn on the campus of Villanova University, and I was excited to be a part of it, but I didn't win a championship by earning the starting spot. Villanova wasn't the school I thought it was during my visit, but I was making the best of it. Some people said I was lucky or that I overachieved by getting into Villanova. People on the outside looking in said I had it made in the shade because I was a student on the Main Line. What they didn't know was that I was flying by the seat of my pants in my new environment.

I slowly integrated by staying positive, just being myself, and walking with my head up and with a smile. I socialized with as many classmates without my background as I did with those who grew up like me. I had a great relationship with Nate, as well as Veltra Dawson, a freshman on the basketball team from Highland Park, Illinois. There were more Black athletes in my dorm than any of the other dorms on campus, and I took advantage by building friendships with each of them—Chip Jenkins, Martin Booker, John Marshal from the track team, and Harold Pressley and Dwight Wilbur, members of the basketball team.

There were no Black upperclassmen football players that I could identify with or who I had shared experiences with socially or culturally. But that was okay because I didn't have any problems making friends, and my confidence as an athlete had grown from the first day I stepped off the train. I was constantly learning about my new environment, and I relied on seniors who I identified with to show me the way. I leaned on three guys from the hoops squad: Dwayne "D-Train" McClain, "EZ" Ed Pinckney, and Gary "Gizmo" McLain. The basketball program reigned supreme over the football program on campus and in the community. Not only was basketball the second religion on our Catholic campus, but I also discovered that college basketball in the Philadelphia Tri-State area towered over college football.

I lived in the same dorm with EZ Ed, Gizmo and D-Train lived in Austin Hall. All three players took on an important role in contributing to the team's success, and each played a very special role in my development on campus. I looked up to and admired them for different reasons.

D-Train was smart and talented off the court. He smashed all the stereotypes of the "dumb jock." He enjoyed reading and music and was well versed on any topic. I noticed how comfortable he was holding a conversation with all our classmates. Gizmo encouraged me to be true to myself, cherish where I came from, but enjoy and embrace where I was. Although EZ was quiet and soft-spoken on the surface, his calm leadership didn't go unnoticed by me, and when it was time to raise his voice, he did it with ease. We shared in the fact that our families were led by women. Our friendship quickly developed into a big brother/little brother relationship. I watched how each senior interacted with other classmates and people in the community from all races, and I hoped I would be as comfortable in my Villanova environment by the time I reached my senior year.

Whenever I had the chance to hang with my upperclassmen brothers, I did. I met their friends outside of sports. One of EZ's classmates, Warren Bishoff, was tall, loud, full of energy, and White. He seemed to like saying my name because he added more names to it. If I saw Warren around campus or in the dorm, he'd yell out Bo-Dachious, Bo-Diddley, or Bo-Smack. At first, I didn't know if he was trying to get a positive or negative reaction out of me or if this was simply part of his personality. Nonetheless, he was starting to get on my nerves. Instead of confronting him about it, I patiently waited to see how long it would continue.

One night, I went upstairs to EZ's room to hang out and Bishoff was there, reliving the first few weekends of the team's success during the NCAA tournament. Bishoff started up again, and I gave him my "you're ticking me off look." He immediately told me he loved my name and he didn't mean anything by it. EZ agreed and confirmed Bishoff did the same with him. Later that night, I thought about how most people from my neighborhood down south received a nickname. It was pretty much the same way, so from that time on, Bishoff was a cool dude to me.

As with this example, adjusting to my new environment required continued effort on my part, and I was willing to do it because I wanted to be there. I was there for a reason. My position coach asked me to host a recruit during the basketball team's 1985 NCAA tournament run. It was part of my responsibilities during spring practice, and I took it seriously. My job was to host a recruit around campus, take him out to eat, and introduce him to as many teammates and friends as possible. I remember what it felt like when "Happy" hosted me on my unofficial visit to Villanova. I wanted to make it just as welcoming—the best visit possible—for the recruit.

I met Bobby Dais in the football office, and I quickly learned he knew more about Villanova than I did. He was from the local area (Aston, PA) and had played for Chichester High. I had a good feeling about him, and I was happy the program was trying to recruit more players that looked like me. For Bobby, Villanova was close to home, and the academic standards were especially important to him. Whether or not he decided to come to Villanova was out of my hands, but I hoped he planned to come. The only problem I had was hosting a potential scholarship athlete, and no scholarship had been offered to me after making the team in the fall and earning a starting spot on defense. I assumed it would be offered at the end of the spring semester. However, I put it in the back of my mind to deal with later.

After hosting the recruit for most of my weekend and hanging out late with my crew on Sunday night, Monday morning came quickly. I wasn't a sleep-in-late type of guy, so I didn't expect the cafeteria to be basically empty when I arrived for breakfast. Going to class was not part of my plan because I didn't want to miss any of the parties leading up to the game. Then a few of the guys in my dorm returned from their early classes, one after the other, confirming that classes were canceled all day. I felt some measure of relief because I had missed more classes during March than I had my entire academic career (high school and Cheyney). I knew I was being too cavalier with my academics. It was Madness on campus, but my plan was to make up for it during my final exams.

I didn't remember the date because the only thing I thought about was our chances of winning the National Championship. I talked myself into believing we had a chance of beating the Georgetown Hoyas because I'd seen it done before in sports. A team loses to another team multiple times during the year or for a long period of time and then one day, the losing team finds a way to win. Most people outside the Villanova family believed there was no way on God's green Earth we had a chance of winning that game. The media referred to our team as the Cinderella team on an improbable journey to the Championship. Everyone on campus was either drinking the "blue" Kool-Aid or living in a "white" bubble, and I was one of them.

After receiving the news about having no classes for the day, I decided to hang in my room and listen to the radio for a while before spring football practice and before the craziness started. One of my favorite songs was playing, "Distant Lover" by Marvin Gaye. The DJ was paying tribute to the legend. I had completely forgotten that it had been one year before, on April 1, when Marvin Gaye had died. I immediately felt mixed emotions because our basketball team was on the cusp of pulling off the biggest upset in recent sports history, and I started to reminisce about where I was, what I was doing, and what I had done that day after the news broke that Marvin Gaye was gone. As I continued to listen to the musical tribute, I thought about my brief time at Cheyney and how grateful I was to get the opportunity to start my college career on the Historically Black campus.

Hours later, it was game time. I watched the game from EZ Ed's room with his girlfriend Rosie, Nate, Buzz, some classmates I knew, some classmates I didn't know, and his friends from the local area. EZ's room was filled with a melting pot of people, all cheering for the same result. Beat Georgetown! I noticed how everyone interacted together, sharing life experiences with one another, and celebrating together because race didn't matter.

After upsetting Georgetown and winning the Championship everyone began to reflect on the incredible championship run the seniors and the team made during the 1985 NCAA Tournament. Our victories during the tournament were special for everyone associated with the basketball program, but it was culturally important for the Black students at Villanova, including me.

During the team's deep run in the tournament, I noticed students on campus were moving toward a utopian society. Winning the Championship didn't cure all the cultural and social differences on campus, but we had a taste of unity for a few weeks and it felt good. From the time the clock hit zero and the Tournament was over, I had accumulated memories that would last forever. I had never experienced winning a championship on any athletic or personal level, so I found myself embracing my new White environment a little more because of the family feeling that spread throughout the campus, and I was proud to bleed blue and white for life.

TOPIC 26. SUMMER CAMP RACE

My summer of 1985 began with a bittersweet feeling. The Villanova alumni, family, friends, local community, Tri-State area, and sidewalk fans around the nation continued to celebrate the April 1 Championship victory. My first year was officially over, yet I had not met all my freshman requirements. I needed to focus on my academics because I had dropped the ball during the Championship race in the spring. It was all on me. I was placed on official academic probation, and my redemption started with the summer sessions. I had to get my eligibility back. I was embarrassed about attending summer school at first because so many athletes stuck around. But I chose not to run from my embarrassment.

Summer camp started out great because so many athletes wanted to be a part of the Villanova experience after winning the National Championship. Athletes came from all over the country to coach. Most, if not all, of the 'Nova basketball players hung around . . . even the four seniors who had just graduated: EZ Ed, D-Train, Gizmo, and Brian Harrington. Most people outside the 'Nova family didn't know there were four seniors on the team, and Brian was the fourth. Although I lived next door to Brian, he and I didn't get the chance to hang out at all during the school year. He was nice, speaking to me every time he saw me. We'd have a short conversation if we met in the hallway, and maybe that was the start of us getting to know each other. I often thought about how he must have felt being the fourth senior on the team but not getting the same level of recognition on campus as the other seniors. I understood the basketball program was "big time," and he didn't get many minutes, but he was part of the team. And I understood that the local media didn't care about how much time he got, but for our classmates not to show him respect on this level, I didn't understand it. I never saw Brian in practice because I'd be walking through the gym headed into the training room or their practice was closed to outsiders, even to the students on campus.

However, during summer camp, I had the chance to spend a little time with Brian and see him play pick-up ball. He was pretty darn good. He was better than the average wannabe ballers that came up to the campus to play pick-up games, and he was on the same level, or better than, most of the summer camp players/coaches that came from other college and university basketball programs. As I started building a stronger relationship with Brian during summer camp, I became frustrated because guys (Black and White) would talk about Brian as if what he contributed to the basketball program didn't matter. It just didn't feel right. I began to develop a little bit of a reputation as the guy who spoke his mind because I would defend Brian whenever someone said anything negative about him. I would call out any Black or White guy that questioned Brian's talent, especially if I played with or against these jealous, backstabbing guys at some point during summer camp. I would question their manhood just to see if they had the courage or the muscle to back up their words in front of me. They didn't. That was the only way I knew how to confront their negative attitudes. I felt that Brian and I had something in common. I had been one of five Black football players on the team during our start-up season, and Brian was the only White player out of four seniors on the Championship team. We were both a minority in a majority place.

Working at the basketball summer camps was a new experience for me. I was working in an athletic environment with Black and White athletes that weren't my teammates. I had never been part of something like it. Parents dropped their kids off at summer camp for a number of reasons, but one of the most important reasons I heard parents say when they dropped their little ones off was to go make lots of friends. I learned a lot and grew personally from working at the summer camps. One such impact (that has remained with me) was that most of the White kids I coached showed me that the next generation wasn't so hung up on race the way most adults were. They wanted as many friends as they could play with and hung out with as many as they could after a long day of camp. And it didn't matter if the other kids were Black or White.

I noticed throughout the camps little White boys and girls having fun with little Black boys and girls. There was a small number of Black kids in the camps. However, I think their exposure had a positive effect on building relationships with their White campmates. White kids roomed with Black kids and coached by Black coaches, and it wasn't a problem. The Black and White kids had the chance to play together and learned the fundamentals of sports. Each kid learned the meaning of teamwork, how to compete, and most importantly, sportsmanship. It was my first opportunity to coach Black and White kids together.

During the overnight camps, I saw Black and White kids rooming together. They were having fun together, and they didn't hold back in any way. They were building a foundation of acceptance and respect for each other. I worked as many summer camps as I could, as long as they didn't conflict with my summer classes. And each of my summer camp experiences was beginning to play a valuable part in my social development.

Each kid had more fun than I did when I attended my first summer camp, and I could see the kids got more out of their camp experiences. The first time I had been around a large group of White athletes was in my one and only football summer camp. I had received the Fellowship of Christian Athlete of the Year award in high school. The camp was in North Carolina, and it had been my first experience traveling out of state. My high school coaches had selected me for the award. I was chosen because I made a personal sacrifice to help the team. I learned each kid attending the camp was recognized as a good kid—a hard worker, coachable, well behaved, and would do anything to help the team. I fit right in because I was told I was that kind of kid. My coach pulled me aside before my trip. "Take it all in, like a sponge."

I remember how excited and nervous I was back then. I was told I would be with kids from all over the country and that included White kids. The only time I ever saw a White kid on the football field was in a different uniform playing for the opposing team. My high school had competed against White teams on the football field. Some were all White teams, and some had a few Black players. So I started my week of youth summer football camp quietly taking it all in. I remember having a good time and meeting kids who loved football and sports, just like me.

Although the summer camp was a short week, I had the opportunity to build pen-pal friendships with some of my White campmates, but I resisted. I viewed my summer camp experience like being on Fantasy Island. The White camp counselors and kids were nice, but I didn't think it was real. Even though all the campers held a belief in God and the love of sports in common, I didn't know how to build relationships, particularly friendships with White people. While growing up in a segregated environment, the opportunity had never presented itself. However, my FCA summer camp experience was a start. The camp had planted the seed in me, but unfortunately, I buried it by the time I had returned home to my Black community, Black school, and Black team because I thought the camp had been a dream. It just seemed so unreal.

TOPIC 27. MYTHICAL RACE

During summer session II, I started to see my PWI in a different light. There were kids everywhere, all the time, day and night. One evening after dinner, EZ Ed wanted to get a workout in because he was a little nervous about starting his new career in the NBA with the Phoenix Suns. He wanted to be in the best physical shape for his NBA team, but no one was around to play ball. I offered to help him workout. During the workout, a kid walked into the gym and his name was Pat, but everyone called him Shorty-G. Every time I saw that little rascal, he was either in the gym or with a basketball player on campus. I assumed he was the son of a Villanova staff member, but he wasn't. He was just a kid that lived in the community and loved Villanova basketball. Shorty G offered to get us in St. Joe's University's gym, where EZ could play or practice with or against other players. As we were driving to St. Joe's, I thought, "How is this little (he was no more than ten or twelve years old) kid going to get us in St Joe's? Who does he know or what does he know that we don't?"

We arrived at the gym, and the kid spoke to the security guards. We couldn't believe it! He got us in.

We entered the gym, and there were two players from the Philadelphia 76ers on the court, Charles Barkley and Sedale Threatt. EZ and Shorty G knew Charles, and of course, I knew *who* he was. They introduced me to both players. Charles and EZ had some history playing against each other. Charles, being the funny guy, immediately starts talking trash to EZ and reminds him of the last butt-kicking he gave EZ and Villanova. I chimed in with, "I'm from J-ville, and I saw the highlights on the news." We decided to play a two-on-two ('Nova vs. 76ers). It was Charles Barkley, 76ers rookie, nicknamed "Round Mound of Rebound," versus "EZ Ed" Edward Lewis Pinckney, the MOP of Villanova's National Championship team and giant slayer of Patrick Ewing from the Georgetown University Hoyas.

When the game started, I saw and felt the mood change. It was go-time. Sedale liked the fact that I was a football player, but he didn't feel the need to prove he was a tough guy. I asked him to teach me a few things (that was my way of talking trash), and he agreed. While the game was a two-on-two competition, the main event was Charles versus EZ, and it was intense, rough, and violent. There was scratching, slapping, elbows, screaming, and yelling. I gained a new respect for pro-b-ball players. My opinion of them had been that they were passive-aggressive and not truly aggressive, like football players. In the end, we lost the game but on a personal level, EZ won because Charles had an outstanding year under his belt as a rookie in the NBA, and EZ withstood all that Charles gave him that night. On our way back to campus, EZ asked Shorty G which team he was rooting for, and the kid replied with something I never heard before. He said, "No one. I love all you guys."

EZ replied, "Cool."

I never heard a White kid say he loved Black people before. I didn't overreact or say anything about it to EZ, ever.

A few days later, we began the next week of summer camp. I walked in the gym, and Mr. Erving was dropping his kids off. I'd never seen anything like it. It was like the Jackson 5 were giving a concert to thousands of people. I saw the looks on the White kids' faces, and I couldn't help but think about the kids in my neighborhood. What would they do if they had a chance to meet Mr. Erving? I had grown up watching Mr. Erving like most of the kids in summer camp. Almost every kid I knew wanted to be "Dr. J," pretending to play like him in parks, driveways, backyards, school gyms . . . even where baskets were nailed up on telephone poles in the street. Kids and adults who played basketball would yell or say the name Dr. J during the game. Kids and adults admired him and everyone (athletes and non-athletes) tried to copy Dr. J's moves—his skywalk, his grace, his style, and even his Afro hairstyle. It was the way he gracefully maneuvered his way through the air, the way he fooled gravity so that he could fly above every defender, and the way he influenced the rock off the backboard and into the rim. And who could forget his "rock the cradle dunk." When the competition went low, he went high, but he never looked down on them. I wasn't a good basketball player as a kid, but my Uncles Billy and Joe spent time with me when they could, teaching me how to play. My Uncle Joe spent more time with me playing the game, and I would go to the park with my uncle and watch him play. Guys on the court would have their Converse shoes on, and most assumed their shoes would help them fly like "The Dr."

My brother wasn't one of the many that idolized Dr. J because he liked Jo-Jo White from the Boston Celtics. I think he liked him because they shared the same nickname, Jo-Jo. One thing the guys at the park could not emulate was Mr. Erving's personality on the court. I never saw Mr. Erving act like the kids or adults at the playground where I grow up: arguing, screaming, or yelling at each other about every little foul. Well, I did actually see him punch Larry Bird on TV. Everyone talked about it, and people made it out to be a racial thing. Most Black people assumed Larry Bird used a racial slur or said something about Mr. Erving's mother. Those were the only reasons my Black teammates or Black classmates could come up with that would cause Mr. Erving to punch Larry Bird during the game. Mr. Erving didn't come across as a hothead or a guy with a short temper. He was classy, professional, and a man with honor.

I grew up in an era when Black athletes had to walk a tightrope, and White athletes did not need to do the same. When Black grandmothers and mothers saw Mr. Erving on TV, they would say, "That's who you want to be like and how you want to behave."

I was amazed at how people who didn't look like me reacted to seeing Mr. Erving. From time to time, I would get a call from Mr. or Mrs. Erving to watch the kids for a little while, and I did. I ran to their house if the weather was nice, or they would pick me up if there was snow on the ground. When they drove over to pick me up, a few of the guys in my dorm would watch from their windows to see if Mr. Erving was the one in the Range Rover or Benz.

Sometimes, I would encounter that "excited classmate," knocking on my room door, saying with either sarcasm or disbelief that Julius Erving (or Turquoise Erving) was on the phone for me. Some would follow me to the phone, as if they had to use the other phone in the hall, to listen to my conversation.

Having had the opportunity to spend a little time with the Erving family had an impact on me. I was able to see the respectful relationship that Mr. Erving and his 76ers teammate, Mr. Bobby Jones, had for each other, and it influenced me to consider "dropping my guard" more and more in my new environment, but I had a long way to go. I saw Mr. Erving's and Mr. Jones's special relationship up close: how they greeted each other, how they acknowledged each other, and the respect as teammates they displayed while having a conversation. It didn't take much time if you were paying attention. I could see both men were unafraid to acknowledge and live out their friendship. It was more than their love of basketball, although I assumed basketball had a lot to do with it. I didn't see or feel racial tension on the surface of their relationship. It was a show of respect. Was their close relationship a result of playing sports together or winning the '83 NBA Title as teammates? I didn't know, but it was an incredible thing to witness, at least for me.

TOPIC 28. POLICE RACE

I had no plans to return home for the full summer because I didn't want to be that young Black man at the wrong place at the wrong time. I heard many stories about athletes hanging out with friends, high school classmates, or someone from the neighborhood and their lives ending with violence. I'd heard enough of those stories. Again and again, college student or athlete shot and killed being at the wrong place at the wrong time or being at the right place at the wrong time.

Although our campus had fewer students on it for the summer, the campus was filled with summer camp kids from all over the United States. The kids were attending football, men's and women's basketball, volleyball camps, and more and that meant campus security would still be everywhere and in full force. I didn't have a problem with campus security because I respected them, and they showed me the same respect. And the one encounter (a traffic stop) I had with the local police didn't turn out to be the death of me. However, one summer night, my life would change forever. It began on a Friday morning when D-Train had to suddenly leave for Indiana to sign his NBA contract with the Indiana Pacers. Veltra told me that D-Train had given him the keys to his rental car for the weekend. D-Train asked Veltra to return the rental to the agency on Monday morning. They were expecting it. Now the Veltra I knew was very sharp, self-absorbed, and would never let a great opportunity slip through his fingers.

The evening began as any other innocent night began. I met Veltra in the main campus "Pit" for dinner, and then went back to the dorm to relax for a few minutes. We changed clothes to work out in the weight room, played hoops in the Field House, and then headed back to the dorm. The music was loud, as it was to be expected on a Friday night, and everyone we noticed was in a great mood. The dorm was jumpin'. All types of music filled the air (rap, rock, R&B, pop, and even country).

After we got dressed in our Miami Vice outfits, we raced to the rental car, a convertible Chrysler, with cigars in hand. Winning was presenting a lot of perks for Veltra, and I was along for the ride. We were feeling like we could do no wrong. We were excited about our new-found freedom and independence. Freedom and independence from our parents (warning us to be careful all the time), our older brothers, the guys we looked up to (trying their best to keep us in line), and from our coaches, always looking over our shoulders (questioning every move we made). It was an independence a large number of our White classmates enjoyed by being able to move about whenever, and however they wanted to— with or without a car.

The top was down and the music blasted from the speakers. It felt good. We were singing the entire ride as we made stops up and down the Main Line. We started at Smokey Joe's, made our way to Kelly's, then to Al 'E' Gators, and ended our Main Line experience at Friendly's. At every spot we entered, the crowd would yell, "'Nova's in the house!"

Then it was time to make our way to City Line Ave. to TGI Friday's. Friday's was the starting point of "The City of Brotherly Love." We had finally made it into Philly. We cruised Delaware Avenue and made our way to South Street. Delaware Avenue and South Street were the heartbeats of the nightlife in Philly. You could buy whatever you needed, eat whatever you wanted, drink whatever adult beverage you liked, and see much, much more. We drove up and down South Street as if we didn't have a care in the world. We'd stop from time to time and talk to the ladies. Most of the time, the ladies wanted to get in the car with us. "Sorry ladies, it's a convertible," Veltra would say. "Not enough room unless you want to sit in our laps." I would have given any of the ladies a ride, but Velta was a little vain. It was all about him that night.

We were a few minutes from returning to our Main Line campus when it seemed like fifty cop cars rolled up on us. They came out of nowhere and surrounded us. The cop cars were in front of us, in back of us, and on both sides of us. They stopped us in our tracks on South Street, and the chaos began, and it was real. It was more terrifying than what I'd seen on TV. The yelling started and everything went from zero to one hundred in seconds. I didn't close my eyes, but everything went black and the noise went silent. I could hear my mom's voice in prayer "Lord, protect him." I recalled everything she taught me. I could hear her voice clearly in my head saying, "Do what they tell you, don't make any sudden movements, don't look angry, and for goodness sake, don't talk back." I also applied the techniques I had learned on the football field. I took a deep breath to slow my mind and heart rate down because it was all happening so fast. I made eye contact with the closest police officer, the one on my side of the car, to make sure I wasn't shot back to his devil. I read the words coming out of his mouth because my hearing hadn't caught up with my eyes. I finally heard the yelling officer say, "Hands up," and another voice over his shoulder yelling, "Out of the car!" Then, "Put them on the car," and from Veltra's side of the car, he thinks he heard the same.

Veltra got out of the car asking questions. "What did we do? Did we run a red light?" The more he opened his mouth and spoke, the louder the chaos became and the more intense it got. It was pure and raw, like a scene from some "cops and robbers" movie. I couldn't believe what I was hearing and seeing from Veltra. I had a decision to make. I could let one of my best friends continue asking questions and put himself in jeopardy of being shot dead or do something against better judgment. I tried to calm him down by asking him to look at me instead of the police guns pointed at us. I called Veltra's name—it seemed like a million times—trying to get his attention so I could tell him to stop talking. He acted as if he'd never come in contact with the police before or as if he'd never had the conversation with his parents about what to do if ever stopped by the police. He finally said something that got the attention of one of the police officers.

Veltra yelled, "I play ball for Villanova!" At that moment, the level of intensity dropped. I could finally breathe fresh air, and the smell of death all around me disappeared. What we had just experienced was more than mayhem! It was close to becoming an unjustified murder. During those moments of madness, I completely understood what DWB (driving while Black) meant, but this was my first time living it. While I was being handcuffed and still looking down the barrel of a gun, a crowd of people stopped to see what was going on. Veltra continued to ask questions, but this time we got some answers. We were told that the rental car was reported stolen by the agency. We stated our case by telling the officers everything we knew and provided the necessary identification. One officer checked the glove box and reviewed the paperwork. He looked a little surprised and pulled one officer over for a private conversation. I assumed he saw D-Train's legal name on the paperwork and came to the conclusion we were who we said we were and how we had possession of the car. While more police huddled for their conversation, more people walked by to see what was going on.

The police discussion ended with Veltra and I being taken to a police station to determine whether our story was true. The scariest thing about our run-in with the police was how out of control Veltra was; he wasn't thinking straight. As we traveled in the very bumpy police wagon, I took the opportunity to yell at Veltra for almost getting us shot. I told him he had panicked and lost his composure.

I could see he was visibly upset, so I took a moment to calm down and gather my thoughts. As we road in the wagon, I thought and assumed, at some point, the police noticed us and ran the car's license plate. I knew we hadn't been speeding or run a red light or committed any infraction. I couldn't put my finger on it. At some point, our conversation turned to whom we were going to call. And in the end, we had no choice but to call Coach Massimino.

We waited in a cell, separate from the other guys, which turned out to be a good sign that things were going in a better direction. The last thing we needed was to share a cell with a few guys that assumed we were soft because we didn't look like we were from Philly. I was in no mood to deal with anyone who didn't bleed blue and white. Before coach Mass arrived, an officer came back to inform us what would happen next. He told us that the car was reported stolen because there was a misunderstanding between the person who rented the car and the rental agency. We would soon be free to go, and there would be no negative record to follow us. Coach Mass arrived to pick us up. Velta sat in the front seat, and I sat in the back of the Cadillac. Velta did all the talking. Even though it was no one's fault, Coach Mass wasn't happy.

With that, my summer was officially over.

TOPIC 29. CAGED RACE

I began my second year on the academically ineligible list and not on the list of players printed in the football program. I was without a team and my dream was fading more and more every day. Although Nate was done with football, he and Velta did their best to keep my spirits up, but Veltra was dealing with his own issues concerning his highly recognized freshmen teammates who were recruited to replace EZ, D-Train, and Gizmo. Velta pushed me to keep my head up and stay in the game mentally. At the same time, he was planning his exit from the basketball program, and I couldn't talk him out of it. I didn't want to give up on my dream, but I didn't know if anyone on campus cared enough other than a few of my Black friends. The biggest problem I faced was not having enough money to pay for the fall semester because I was ineligible. I assumed I had missed my scholarship opportunity. It kept me up every night for days.

I finally called my godmother and she directed me to the Financial Aid office. She told me to park myself in or outside that office every day and ask for help. I hesitated but did it anyway. I assumed no one would care because I was no longer an active player dressed in blue and white and representing the university, but I parked myself in the FA office day after day until the staff got tired of seeing me.

Finally, I met with the Financial Aid Director, Jean Fazio, and she was amazing. She treated me like she cared about my problem, and she provided solutions to my problems. My godmother and Ms. Fazio spoke the same language. They spoke so much they began to build a good relationship. I had the opportunity to sign up for the work-study program, and I took advantage of it. I had the option of working in the Athletic Department or the Connelly Center.

I picked the Athletic Department to stay close to the action. I spoke to the Assistant A.D. Jim Brown, and he pointed me in the direction of Bobby Lambert the equipment manager and the man in charge of the cage. (The equipment office was called the cage.) I was glad that working with Mr. Lambert was an option for me because all my former teammates liked and respected him. I met with Mr. Lambert in his office and before I could tell him my story, he already knew the details. He asked me to work for him and his assistant managers with a few conditions. First, show up for the time I signed up for, and second, he was going to stay on top of me when it came to my schoolwork. I agreed and gave him my word I would do my best. All the athletes stopped by the cage before and after practices and games.

Mr. Lambert's assistants were Mr. Bob Geary and Mr. Don DiCarlo. I didn't know Mr. Geary that well but he was a cool guy, and I knew Mr. DiCarlo Sr. because his son had been my teammate the previous year but decided not to participate in spring practice. Mr. DiCarlo was Italian and the ramrod of the group. He was a former Marine and local police officer. He loved football and the wishbone office used by southern and mid-west football programs. He got on me about everything, but I was able to adjust to him because he was very similar to my position coach, whom Mr. DiCarlo liked very much. Mr. DiCarlo would say, "If you're not working on cage business here, you better be working on your homework or preparing for a test." Don Jr. was very smart, and I began to see why. Mr. DiCarlo didn't accept any excuses. The cage became more than a place where I showed up to work. Mr. Lambert, Mr. Geary, and Mr. DiCarlo taught me and motivated me to get back on track with my academics.

The football season was over, and I was on track to regain my eligibility at the end of the semester. Christmas was around the corner and basketball season was in full swing. I had a decision to make—spend money to go home or stay on campus and work through the holidays. I decided to stay. I couldn't afford to live on campus during the spring semester, so I used the time off to look for a place off-campus. And I was lucky; a few of my friends—Buzz and Nate, the two celebrities of our crew, Big Lou, the first black man I've ever met with green eyes, and Rob, (a.k.a. Throb, who never had a problem finding a date)—decided to move off-campus as well. We moved down the street from campus and called our place the crib.

Just before Christmas break, I was offered help moving out of my dorm by one of my classmates. Kathleen Tuny Cory overheard me talking about moving in with my crew of friends. I had noticed her in class. She was friendly but overly talkative. On occasion, I had thought to myself, "This White girl never shuts up." But she offered, and I needed the help, so I accepted. I never in my life met anyone, Black or White, like her. Tuny, as we called her, was tiny and said whatever was on her mind, no matter the topic. She got along with all my friends, and she wasn't uncomfortable around Black people.

During the holiday break, a couple of things happened that took me by surprise: I was invited to have dinner with Mr. DiCarlo and his family, and Tuny wanted me to meet her mother. I'd never been to a White person's home before. I didn't know what type of food would be prepared. I struggled with the invitations, but I decided to accept both.

My off-campus housing was very close to Mr. DiCarlo's home. From the time I walked in Mr. D's home, I didn't feel like a guest, I felt like family. It was good to see Don Jr. again, and it was wonderful to meet his wife, Mary Jane, and younger son, Scott, for the first time. There was food everywhere, just like back home when our family got together for the holidays. I thought, "These White folks have a lot in common with Black folks." Mr. D. pointed out all the different Italian meats, sandwiches, and poppers. I was concerned I'd get agita from tasting all the appetizers, and I wouldn't have any room for dinner. It wasn't Christmas or anyone's birthday or any special day, but it felt like it was.

A few days later, I met Tuny's mother on a day her father was out of town. Ms. Gail qualified as one of the sweetest mothers on the planet. Tuny described the situation to me, and I completely understood. I assured Tuny I felt no different about her because of the situation with her dad, and regardless of how things were, it wouldn't affect our friendship . . . and it never did. I felt blessed to have Tuny as my friend, and I protected her as if she were my little sister; although, she didn't need it because she was a pistol and could hold her own.

The only place I wanted to hang out during the holiday season away from my family was the gym. I became a gym rat and the Field House was my football field with walls. One evening, before the gym shut down for the night, the Supervisor of Custodial Services Tom Riley asked me to watch his kids while he and his staff member, Mr. Al checked out a mechanical issue in the cage. I couldn't believe Mr. Riley (a White man) trusted me to watch his kids, Tom Jr. and Mimi. While we played hoops together, the only thing on my mind was to protect his kids with my life.

Downstairs, under the gym floor, was where the cage was located. I spent so much time doing homework and working out in the Field House and the cage. I knew all the Black athletes, but the cage gave me the opportunity to get to know the White athletes from the other sports, people like Wyatt Maker, Mark Plansky, and R.C Massimino from the men's basketball squad. And from the women's team was one of the best that ever played, Shelly Pennefather. Shelly didn't act as if she was the best in the country, but she was. She was very nice, quiet, soft-spoken, and a real baller on the court.

One morning, I was walking to campus and a red Porsche pulled up. The window rolled down, and a voice yelled out, "You need a ride?" I looked in the car, and it was Charles Barkley. He was headed past 'Nova and was happy to give me a ride. I assumed he remembered me from our pick-up game at St. Joe's and from the time Charles became a friend to Villanova.

It was quiet in the cage and the gym during the holiday break. I worked out every minute I could. Later that night, during my workout and playing hoops, I busted my ankle pretty badly. I started out at our on-campus infirmary and later was taken to the local hospital. I had fractured my ankle and would be in a cast for at least six weeks or more. I was so upset with myself because every time I took two steps forward, I ended up taking one step back. I was so mad, I decided to spend Christmas by myself. Mr. DiCarlo yelled at me, and Tuny couldn't understand why I didn't call to tell her about my injury. I told them both it was something I wanted to deal with on my own.

All the athletic administrative offices were in the Field House. Over time, I notice more staff members asking me how I was doing academically and encouraging me to do my best and wishing me well in my recovery, including Academic Advisor Dan Regan, Business Manager Joe Mulligan, SID Craig Miller, Assistant SID Jimmy DeLorenzo, Athletic Support Services, Larry Shane, Intramural Director Andy McGovern, Basketball Secretary Mary Anne Gabuzda, and the woman we (most athletes) called Mom, Joan McGuckin.

After my eight weeks in purgatory, I was back in the gym and chopping at wood to get back on the field for spring practice. Classes had resumed, and I was cleared by the team doctor, Head Athletic Trainer Dan Unger, and his assistant. Fran Raggazino, to start working out again. I promised myself that I was never going to go through that again. I needed to get my legs and lungs back in shape. My workouts were rough, and I pushed myself up and down the basketball court harder than I had ever pushed myself before.

One night, I thought all the administrative staff had gone home for the evening, so I decided to dunk the basketball before I called it a wrap and head home. I needed to test myself. And boom! I dunked the ball, and that's when I knew I was going to be all right.

One minute later, I heard a voice call my name. It was the Director of Marketing, Mr. Bill McDonough. He called me up to his office. I didn't know what to expect because I knew his son. Billy Jr. was a senior in high school and from time to time, he would stop by the crib (more like show up) with his friends to hang out. Billy was a high-spirited kid with a few shenanigans up his sleeve. I didn't think I had done anything wrong, but I was ready for anything to happen. I walked into Mr. McDonough's office, and he asked me to have a seat.

He had heard me during my work out on the court and stepped out of his office to take a look. He knew about my injury, and he was impressed with my ability to recover fast. He noticed me hanging around during the Christmas break, and he admired my dedication. We spent the next half hour discussing my future—my career move—just in case my dream of playing for 'Nova again didn't come true. He told me that with my personality and social skills, I could do or be whatever I wanted to be. He said everyone spoke highly of me and that could carry me a long way, but it was up to me. He finished with, "I know you're friends with my son, but you haven't met my wife and the rest of my kids. You're welcome to come over any time."

As I walked home, I relived the conversation with Mr. McDonough until I reached the crib. I had never felt more liberated to be who I was or more unrestricted to be what I wanted to be. It was two steps forward again—back to being more than *that* athlete with potential, and I was no longer in a cage.

TOPIC 30. BLUE & WHITE RACE

The sky was blue with a few white clouds as I walked from the Connelly Center to the football locker room. My energy level was high because I had a lot to be thankful for. I was officially back on the active roster, and we had a game in a few days. I bumped into my classmate and Ms. Erving's personal assistant along the way. I asked how her mom was doing, and we briefly talked about Mr. Erving's retirement season. She offered to take me to a game or two during the 76ers' season. My focus was on football, so, "Let me get through the football season," I replied. I made it to the locker room, and I sat at the foot of my locker to get some homework done. I was alone, getting excited about wearing the blue and white jersey on game day. I understood how lucky I was because some players stepped away from the game, and others were forced away by injury.

Coach Ferraro elevated me to the second team during the preseason training camp, and I completely understood the reason. I didn't deserve the starting position I had earned two years ago just because I was back with the program, and I understood that a freshman scholarship player was in front of me. During training camp, I played with a level of intensity that surprised even me at times. Craig Johnson, the Quarterback and receivers' coach, walked by me every day during warm-ups, and whispered, "Don't hurt his guys," and then he'd wink and smile. And moments later, Dave White, the Associate Head Coach and running backs coach, did the same and my reply was "You've got Jeff Dingle." I knew coach White was concerned because the day before I knocked the snot out of his starting running back, Ron Sency. While I was on probation, the team went undefeated (5–0), and I was happy for the guys. My expectations were high for our second official season. Our schedule was full with nine games, and I looked forward to playing in as many of them as possible.

The faces on the team started to change, but the ethnic ratio still lagged behind. The program had started with five Black players, and when I returned, the team had fifteen Black players. Although we were a team and everyone appeared to like each other, there were pockets of teammates that hung out together, and I was guilty of it, too. The largest group of Black players (eight) was on defense and the defensive back group (five) outnumbered all the other groups. That made it easy for me to adjust because of our shared experiences and being defensive players. Even though I was more comfortable as a Black student and athlete on campus, I was still a little guarded.

Our first game of the season was on the road and would be my first road trip with the team. We took a bus to the airport, made our way through the terminal, and settled at the gate. The defensive back group was the group everyone seemed to want to hang out with. I walked away from the group to grab a drink, and when I returned, more guys had joined our group. Two from defense (Joe Allen and Bobby Dais) and two from offense (Jeff Dingle and Rich Lage). Joe, Bobby, and Jeff were Black and the odd guy in that group, Rich, was White. We teased and joked around with each other for a little while.

The Airport Terminal. L to R: On a knee, Charles Martin, standing Derek McEwen, sitting Joe Allen, Bo-Dean Sanders, Robert "Bobby" Dais, and Richard "Big Country" Lage.

Later, Jeff returned to hang with his offensive group, but Rich didn't. I thought it was odd that he was still hanging around, and I didn't understand why he wanted to. I noticed he fit in with our group more than he connected with any other White teammate. I butted heads with Rich every day in practice and my gut feeling was that he didn't like me. I thought it was more than offense versus defense. I didn't go out of my way to be friendly with him, and it didn't help that he was from Charlottesville, Virginia and spoke with a deep Southern country accent. So I kept my distance.

Defensive Captain Joe Allen did his best to help team chemistry by making sure everyone had a positive attitude. I talked with Joe for a while, and I learned a few things from him regarding building better relationships with our teammates. Maybe he noticed I wasn't as friendly, open, or talkative when Rich was around.

Before the team boarded the plane, the coaches pulled our groups together and handed out the itinerary for the trip. Coach Ferraro pulled me aside and asked me if I was ready. I replied, "I've never been more ready." I was paired with Bobby Rosato, the starting strong safety, for our hotel room assignment. My first reaction was, "I think I can work with that" because I had time to prepare myself. I liked Bobby because our playing styles were very similar even though we had very different approaches. I sacrificed my body, making the big hits, because I had something to prove, and Bobby made the same sacrifice because it was his job. We tagged Bobby with two nicknames; one was "Mad-Dog" and the other was "Kamikaze." After arriving at the airport, checking into the hotel, and preparing for the game the next day, it was time for a bed check by the coaching staff. Time to call it a night.

Bobby and I talked for a while, and I learned more about my teammate. On our first night as roommates, Bobby wanted to sleep with the lights out, and I didn't. He turned the light out and I turned it back on a few minutes later. This went on for a half-hour until he asked me if I was reading my playbook. In response, I referred to stories I had heard about hotels having spiders and bugs, and if people kept the lights on, the light would keep them away. He looked at me as if I was out of my mind. So we compromised and turned the TV on for the night. I told him that crazy and bizarre story because I didn't have any experience rooming with him. And, I didn't fully trust him yet.

I roomed with Bobby for both away games at the start of the season. I quickly felt more comfortable with him as my road trip roommate. Plus, I could tell that dude was flat out crazy, and I grew to love that about him. I hoped he would be my roommate for the Catholic University game in Washington, D.C. I had circled that game on the schedule because I was friends with Marie-Claire Woodring, a student at Georgetown University.

Marie-Claire was from the local Main Line, and we had met during the summer. Her sister was friends with an athlete on the basketball team who was from Canada, and he happened to be White. I had been invited with a few other guys to Marie-Claire's home a few times to swim in their family pool and have lunch. Her family treated me with respect and accepted me with open arms. Marie-Claire's father was a well-known ear, nose, and throat doctor in the area. They reminded me of the Walton Family, from the TV show, except the upper-class version. Marie-Claire attended the game with a few of her classmates. It was the first game I left tickets at the will call window for anyone to see me play. Bobby played his consistently outstanding game, and I played the best game of my career. From that point on, I continued to play well and was living my dream.

Bobby, Brian (the scholarship freshmen), and I ended the season being known as the killer B's. How poetic. During the season we rotated playing time so much I felt like the starting spot was in my reach. We finished the season with an 8–1 record. Our program was on its way to getting the attention it had once earned from a few of our doubting classmates, the local media, and local football programs, such as Temple, Penn, and the Delaware Blue Hens. I had never experienced a football season like my return season.

Meanwhile, Bobby was on schedule to graduate at the end of the year. I looked forward to spring practice and competing for that starting spot against Brian Reed. I often ran into coaches on campus away from the gym and most would engage in small talk. But Coach Ferraro was all business all the time. I'd never known him to cross the line between coach and player. I ran into him at one of the local pizzeria spots, and he pulled me aside for a short conversation. I hoped he wanted to talk to me about scheduling some time to discuss a scholarship (partial or full) because of my contribution during the season. And I was going to need a place to live in the fall because our lease was up at the end of the semester. It took me by surprise, and I was shocked by what he told me.

I would be coached by him for the last time. He was leaving our program to coach somewhere else. He stressed how important it was for me to continue to work hard on my academics and receive my degree from 'Nova. I appreciated his personal concern for my future, his man-to-man discussion about my academics and my goal to graduate from 'Nova. And that was the last time I spoke to him before he left the program.

It took me a few weeks before I came to grips with his leaving. I had developed a unique relationship with Coach Ferraro. He allowed me to play with passion and emotion. He pulled more out of me than I thought or believed I had. He had such an impact on me, and I considered myself lucky to have been coached by him. I would hear him yelling in my sleep. The volume of his voice vibrated and echoed across the campus. Before I got to 'Nova, I had heard that all White people were the same . . . just like racist people believe that all Black people were the same. I learned from my relationship with Coach Ferraro that he didn't represent all White people and not all White people were the same.

I met the new position coach before spring practice started, and he seemed like a nice guy. I was sure it would be easier to adjust to his style of coaching compared to Coach Ferraro, but initially, he was hard to read. He was low key, not a yeller, and seemed to have no intensity or passion. I quickly learned what he thought of me. Everything I did in practice was wrong and at every turn, he called me out for something. It felt hostile, or at the very least, it felt like he was trying to run me out of town. I wondered if any of my teammates noticed because it was obviously clear to me. I felt he wasn't pushing me to make me a better player because I knew what that felt like. By the time spring practice was over, I was demoted to third team back up for the fall season. I was in no position to complain or transfer to another football program because I had too much time and effort invested at 'Nova at that point. I wasn't going to let him get the best of me or change my attitude or destroy everything I worked hard to accomplish, including my newfound view of White people. I wasn't going to give up or walk away. I was prepared to deal with whatever happened in the fall. I was going to wear my blue and white jersey for my junior season.

CHAPTER V

Embrace Race

TOPIC 31. HOMELESS RACE

During the summer, I worked and saved to pay for my tuition, but I didn't earn enough to pay for room and board. My grades were outstanding during both summer sessions. Preseason camp went as I assumed it would, leaving spring practice. During preseason practice, I lived in the dorms with my teammates, but at the end of preseason, I needed to find a place to live and find the money to pay for it. Mr. D. allowed me to sleep in his office on the couch until I found my way out of the situation.

On the first official day of my junior year, I got up off the office couch, got myself together, and headed straight for Ms. Jean's office. I maintained my Southern hospitality by smiling or saying hello to everyone that crossed my path on campus, even though my mind was on the results of the additional financial aid I needed, and whether Juanita had found any money. As I walked up the steps of Kennedy Hall, I prepared myself for the worst. I walked into the financial aid office, and Ms. Jean was the bearer of sad news. I could see the pain and disappointment on her face. I'd known Ms. Jean for a while, and I was very familiar with her facial expressions.

My godmother was unable to find any additional aid using her resources. Over time, the conversations between Ms. Jean and Juanita grew into a level of respect on both a personal and professional level. I had never seen a White woman hold a Black woman in high regard before, and it got my attention. Ms. Jean always had nice things to say about my godmother anytime I bumped into her around campus. I got the feeling that Ms. Jean was rooting for me, more than she let on. As I walked out of her office, she reminded me to sign up for the work-study program, and she wanted to know what my plan would be next. I told her, "I'll be okay; I'll figure it out." But the truth was I had no idea what I was going to do.

I didn't ask Ms. Jean if she called the Athletic Department or the football office to see if there was any assistance coming from the football program. I should have, but at that point, I knew where they stood. I didn't get angry because I didn't have time to, but I did feel defeated and isolated as an athlete on the football team with other scholarship players. After all, I had proven myself on the field during the previous season. Months of hoping to receive some type of scholarship funds (partial or full) were all for nothing. I felt like the village idiot.

There was no hole deep enough to bury my pain, but I didn't grow up mentally thinking or feeling I was part of a permanent underclass. So I needed to find a way to survive my hardship, and I was determined to fight through it. The situation was unlike when I first arrived on campus, dealing with the overcrowded student body and Father Stack stepping in to help me out. I felt I had used all nine lives that a cat was said to have. I was desperate with no family nearby or safety net in the area to fall back on. I had to consider my options. What do I do next? I didn't know, but what I did know was I was officially homeless.

As a student and athlete attending Villanova, which was located in an affluent and prominent White Main Line community, I was surrounded by the largest estates and mansions I had ever seen in my life. A large number of homes were like the houses on the TV show "Dynasty," and they sat around every outer corner of the campus. These homes were extraordinary, stunning, glamorous, and fabulous places in a community full of wealth and history. Each design and style was more remarkable than the next. From English, French, Italian, Spanish, Victorian, and Tudor to farmhouse, rustic, and contemporary, most of these castles were made from all types of expensive quarry stones, bricks, and other materials. It was a community where the median value of a home was in the millions.

There were luxury condos, townhouses, duplexes, and apartments that were redeveloped to accommodate a large number of college students from the approximately eight colleges on the Main Line. I couldn't afford one on my own, nor could I afford to share a studio apartment with another college student in the area. 'Nova had four or five male dorms on campus, and I couldn't stake my claim inside any of them. Not one room was in my reach. I felt like I was being blocked from living in every dorm I walked past every day during summer training camp because of my lack of funds. I had become a dorm-less refugee and homeless college athlete.

I didn't have time to dwell on it or wallow in my hardship. It was time to get myself into a higher level of survival mode and fight my way out of this mess. I wasn't going to hide or run away from the circumstance because things weren't going my way. I had faced adversity on and off the field most of my life. I was prepared to bet on myself and finish the race I started after high school. For three years, I'd seen teammates and classmates deal with hardships. Most overcome them, and the rest quit. I was determined to overcome mine.

I refused to give up, drop out, and quit. It was time for me to pick up the pieces of my shattered dream and put it back together, but I knew it would look different. It was my choice and a responsibility I owed not only to myself but to my family and friends to fight my way to the end. I also didn't want to go back home and become a statistic or get swallowed up by the streets. Over the years, San, my "Irish-Twin" kept me updated on my high school teammates, classmates, and neighbors whose lives ended too soon.

I worked very hard to fight through my own self-inflicted wounds and barriers to stay at 'Nova when it got tough, regardless of who or what caused those barriers. I had enough people on campus (some Black but more were White) helping me push through those barriers time after time. And I wasn't going to let anybody down either. I was prepared to do whatever I needed to make it through, but I wondered, "How am I going to do it? Was I going to live on the street? Was I going to be found sleeping in the tunnel under the Norristown High-Speed Line/Stadium train stop or under the Paoli R5 Amtrak Regional Rail near the first dorm (St. Mary's) I was assigned for my freshman year? Would I be seen aimlessly wandering around campus because I needed shelter from the rain? Would I use the money in my pocket or the small amount of money in my checking account to check into a hotel room on brutally cold nights?

I didn't own a car to sleep in or to use to commute back and forth if I lived in the local area. And there was no way on God's green Earth I could commute from Pennsylvania to Florida and back. Villanova was 883 miles away from my front door in Jacksonville. Maybe I'd become that person going to class with the bulging back sack, carrying everything I owned from one class to the next. Or would I be the person people ignored because I represented the problem of homelessness? All I knew, I was now an athlete with no dorm to call home.

My future was no longer certain. It seemed as if my dream was being ripped away and about to vanish. I refused to think about going back home. I wasn't scared to return home, but I would be enraged if I had to because I was so close to completing one of my dreams. I was not going to drop out. I would never forgive myself if I gave in to that thought because I would be announcing to everyone that I had quit. And I didn't want to be known as someone who quits.

I walked to the Connelly Center after leaving Ms. Jean's office. I was mentally and physically exhausted. Partially from the hard-preseason training camp but mostly the emotional stress that weighed on me as a non-scholarship athlete. It was late morning, and I needed something to eat. I pulled my hands out of my pocket, and I had more than enough for a late breakfast. I sat at a table thinking about what to do next and talking to classmates as they returned to school for the year.

One classmate had a look on her face that I was a little familiar with. It was the same one I had when I arrived at 'Nova on my first day. She looked confused, not happy. I was definitely confused, but I wasn't unhappy. I offered to help, and she accepted. She needed to register for classes and needed help finding a few buildings. At the end of the conversation, she had a smile on her face, and I felt good for helping her out. The conversation took my mind off my troubles for a while.

I headed to the Pavilion to see Mr. DiCarlo and let him know I was signed up for work-study again. I tried to control my emotions by forcing myself to smile more than normal because I knew Mr. D. was going to ask if the football program gave me any money, and once I told him the outcome, he would go ballistic. I also knew how much Mr. D. loved football, and in my mind, having someone connected to the football program was important to him. I guess I didn't do a good enough job of hiding my disappointment because when he saw me, he immediately blew his top.

I had learned over the years that my Italian boss was full of emotion. I was all too familiar with his way of expressing his feelings about any and everything. And while he was blowing his top, I found myself interrupting him by assuring him I was okay, and I would work it out.

"I just need a day or two," I said.

At that moment, I realized how much he cared about me. I'd seen him over the years lose his cool, and I knew when issues mattered and when they didn't. My issue mattered to him because he knew what it meant to me and how difficult it was going to be for me to stay in school without additional financial assistance.

I was like a family member to him, one who had just received bad news, and that bad news was felt throughout the entire family. Mr. D.'s reaction became one more of the many moments demonstrated by a White person caring about my wellbeing as a person and not just as an athlete. And those moments were all adding up. After Mr. D. calmed down, he reminded me of the most important thing.

"Finish school," he said. "You've got to find a way to finish school."

TOPIC 32. ROOMMATE RACE

I went to practice and acted as if nothing was wrong. My position coach never asked me how I was doing, asked where I was living, or showed any interest in my total wellbeing. Being homeless was a heavy burden on my mind. I gave it everything I could in practice, but I was probably just going through the motions on the field that day. I watched as my teammate who played the same position took most of the reps. I completely understood. He was on full scholarship, and I wasn't.

I watched the back-up safety (not sure if he was on scholarship or not) get the remaining reps on the field. I was being phased out. I thought to myself, "I know I'm not on scholarship and it's possible I may not be head over heels better than my two teammates, but I know I'm on the same level." I had a gut feeling my playing time was going to get worse during training camp. So the only time on the field for me would be on special teams. Special teams would be where I decided to hang my hat and hammer some nails in the coffin of my opponents during the games if I got the chance to play.

I had to refocus. I remembered what Coach Ferraro had told me before he left the program and what Mr. D. had told me that morning. "Finish school." My plan was to do just that, but it was going to be easier said than done. I had to change my mind-set and reshape my heart from the image of a football to the image of a college degree. My focus in class had to be on the same level it was back when I needed to improve my grades to get back on the field.

After my late class, I walked to Stanford Hall. Most of my teammates were assigned there for the year. I figured I would kill some time by hanging out with a few of them before I went back to Mr. D.'s office for the night. On my way to the dorm, I ran into my teammate, Bobby D. He was known around campus as one of the nicest athletes and an all-around great person. Bobby and I had developed a good friendship during his first two years. I played a small part in his decision as a high school recruit to attend 'Nova. I came to know him as a stand-up guy. Bobby and I had a few things in common. We were both defensive players, both back-ups on the playing field, and both not happy about it. But we didn't make a lot of noise around campus or complain about it, nor did we stop supporting our teammates!

I eventually told him my bad news and without hesitation, he invited me to crash in his room until I figured things out. I said, "No," but he insisted. He wouldn't take no for answer. Bobby's roommate was also our teammate and that made it a little easier for Bobby to make the offer he did. My plan was to ask his roommate once we got to his room, but Bobby said, "Don't worry about it, we're all defensive players, and we've got each others' backs."

I thought, "We're all Black, and we should have each others' backs."

Bobby and I relaxed for a while. We talked about our families and the classes we were taking. When Bobby's roommate returned, he was with a young lady. Bobby explained my situation and asked if I could hang until I worked things out. Both agreed to me crashing in their room for a few days. I never doubted that my teammates would help me out, and I assumed they would because they were Black. A few of my Black teammates and I felt the need from time to time to express our support for one another by saying, "I got your back."

I gathered a few of my things from Mr. D.'s office with Bobby's help, which gave our teammate some time with his date. Later that night, the three of us talked for a while. The next day, I continued searching for a solution to my homeless problem. I checked out potential options and resources, but none panned out. That night, I went to the Connelly Center to continue thinking about my next move. My plan was to stay busy until it was time to head back to the dorm and call it a night. I was prepared to do this for only a few days and nights so my teammates wouldn't feel I was becoming a burden.

On the third night, I started to feel like I was reliving the same day over and over again, so, I went back to the room a little early. Bobby wasn't there but my other teammate was, hosting another female guest.

I quickly apologized and said, "I'll come back later." I knew she wouldn't be there long because the university had a curfew for the male and female dorms. I went upstairs to visit two other Black teammates on the second floor. One was a homeboy from the South (the Dirty South) and a fellow defensive back, Xavier Hargrove, nicknamed X-man. Xavier was born and raised in Florida for a short time but moved to Atlanta. Jeff Dingle, his roommate, was from Hempstead, Long Island, and in his second year as a running back. X-man and JD were in their room listening to music and completing homework. They were happy to see me but surprised at the same time. Both thought I had a room somewhere on the main campus.

I gave them the full story, and they were surprised to find out that Bobby or his roommate hadn't said anything to them. We talked for a while, and I learned a little more about them. What I knew about my teammates from the locker room, on the sideline, in practice, or during a game, wasn't the same as spending time with them away from the field of play. I was again offered a place to crash by my Black teammates for a few days until I figured something out. I took them up on their offer because we all agreed that Bobby's roommate was a lady's man, and I didn't want to cramp his style.

On my fourth night of being homeless, I poked my head in the room of Rich Lage and Perry Hodge next door to JD and X. They were my teammates and they were definitely from the other side of the ball. Both Rich and Perry were offensive players and White. Something in my gut moved me to stop, knock, and say hello. Rich's father had passed away during the summer while a few of us were in summer session on campus, and the word hadn't spread until the entire team returned for preseason summer camp. I had faced Rich every day in practice the previous year. He was a little different this year, and he had every right to be with the loss of his father.

I didn't know Perry well, and at that moment, I took the opportunity to get to know him. Perry was a freshman, our starting punter, and the third-string QB (quarterback). We spoke on the practice field during preseason training camp and in the locker room as we walked past each other, but we had very little interaction off the field.

I knocked on their door and said, "Yo! How you guys doing?" Rich replied, "What's up Bo-Bo," and Perry said, "Come in Bo-Dean." Rich knew I had crashed next door, in X-man and Jeff's room, the night before because he came right out and told me as much.

I explained why I was next door and what my next steps would be. I didn't know why I told Rich and Perry my situation, but I did, and without thinking about it for a second Rich said, "You can stay here if you want."

And Perry said, "Yeah Bo-Dean, anything we can do to help."

And before I could let my pride and stupidity get in the way because they were White and say, "No thanks" or "I'm okay with staying next door," Rich said, "Heck, you can stay all year. I don't give a darn; we Southerners gotta stick together," and Perry enthusiastically agreed.

I couldn't believe it, and maybe I had a look of shock on my face because my teammates were waiting for me to say something—anything. Before I could reply with, "Are you sure?" Perry said, "Where's your stuff? I'll help you move in." I was blind-sided that Rich would offer to help because of the hardship and grief he was dealing with, and I was amazed that a freshman would jump at the chance to help an upperclassman. But more importantly, two White teammates . . . that was unexpected.

Perry didn't know me or have any shared experiences or connections or time on the practice field with me as Rich did. He could have easily punted on the opportunity to help back to our Black teammates next door (JD and X), but he didn't. I told Rich and Perry that I didn't have much next door, and I had a few items in Mr. D.'s office in the Pavilion. I grabbed my things from next door while I gave them the news. Jeff Dingle gave me a hug and went next door to thank the guys for helping me out. Jeff was a nice guy, but his reaction definitely surprised me. I wasn't surprised that Jeff was a nice guy. I knew him as a gentleman, honorable, and very intelligent. JD was a young man with great character. What surprised me was his level of comfort with Perry and Rich.

I headed to the Pavilion and JD insisted on tagging along to help grab the rest of my belongings. As we walked and talked, I got to learn his views on campus life and how deeply he felt about a number of topics. JD expressed how much he liked Perry and Rich. JD had more confidence in my new living situation than I did. He said something to me that stuck with me for a while. "You have what it takes to persevere, and everything will work out."

As we walked past Bartley Hall and the Field House, I thought, "This kid is incredibly mature for an underclassman," and in my mind, he was now on my list of one of the super-smart brothers on the 'Nova campus.

It took one trip to pick up the rest of my things (I didn't own much) from Mr. D.'s office and move into Rich and Perry's room. I don't remember how I got my hands on a red futon to sleep on, but once Perry saw it, he fell in love with it because it matched his red sports car. I got settled in the room, and we talked late into the night. While we talked, the pressure of being homeless started to fade away. I didn't set out to violate the dorm rules, and I didn't want that enormous burden as their refugee roommate on my teammate's shoulders, but they were more than happy to take the risk.

TOPIC 33. SOUTHERN RACE

I was one of three roommates/athletes from three different former Southern Confederate states, three religious principles, three economic backgrounds, and three different ages, sharing a small dorm room. Three was going to be more than a crowd. I assumed it could be difficult as roommates (one Black and two White) from three former slave states trying to live together as roommates. Rich, Jr. was from Charlottesville, Virginia, a Lutheran from a stable middle-class family, age twenty and standing at six feet, five inches and 230 pounds. He spoke with a strong Southern accent, as if he grew up on the ponderosa, with a cut and dried, no bull crap, and no-nonsense personality.

Perry was from the plantation and Low country area of Hilton Head, South Carolina, Episcopalian, with (I assumed) an affluent background, age seventeen, six feet, three inches and 210 pounds. Perry possessed a nice, approachable, down-to-earth personality and was maybe just a little wet behind the ears. Perry was filled with a spunky energy and traditional Southern manners. He oozed Southern hospitality with a slightly less Southern accent than Rich. I didn't know if my Florida culture, Southern Baptist upbringing, low-income background, positive personality (some would say slightly arrogant), and stubborn attitude at age twenty-two or my six feet, two-inch, 195-pound frame could fit in or mix with my new White roommates.

Although I had some experience rooming with Whites during a summer football camp, when I first arrived at 'Nova, and with a teammate on the road during the previous football season, I never imagined I would be rooming with two White guys for more than a month or two, and I knew living next door to a White classmate was not the same as living with a White person. From the start, I didn't know if our personalities would clash, but I knew we were coached to love your teammates and have your teammates' backs. We were a unit, so I knew we had a shot at making it work.

My experience had taught me that statement was easier said than done, sometimes. After all, I had done everything to enhance my relationships at my PWI and the White, affluent community I was in. I was faced with my biggest test socially, and I needed to dig and reach deeper inside myself to be as equally fair to my new White teammates as roommates, as I was to my Black teammates, Black roommates, and Black friends on and off campus. I was a little concerned because you never know someone until you're behind closed doors with him. I hoped the horrible parts of our Southern Black and White past history hadn't followed us to 'Nova. I hoped the seeds of the Jim "coward" Crow system—mistrust, dishonesty, stereotypes, racial anxiety, and loyalty to our race (Black or White)—were not planted in our hearts, minds, and souls. I had to move past our Black and White histories, the negative part of history people wanted us not to forget, and the history of Blacks and Whites not getting along. I made the decision to focus on my positive experiences, not the negative ones, that I'd had with so many people on campus over time. I had to totally get out of my own way, and I hoped my new roommates were prepared to do the same.

In order to get to know my roommates better, I knew our conversations needed to start with what we had in common because we were from different fragments of the South. I knew we had one obvious thing in common—the love of sports, specifically football. I didn't want to be too talkative from the start, but I knew I needed to make the effort to get to know my new roommates and teammates better. I was the curmudgeon in the group with the most on-campus and life experiences in the room. I didn't want awkward silence to be part of our downtime. Rich was the guy with a dry (but funny) sense of humor and told it as he saw it, and Perry was filled with youthful excitement. Perry viewed our living situation as if we were having a big sleepover. So my plan was to choose the right time to start a conversation but not force it.

I met Rich on the football field my first season back after being academically ineligible. Rich was the back-up tight end. He and I literally butted heads every day in practice because of the positions we played, and our battles were epic. He thought I was arrogant, cocky, and a loud jerk. He called it as he saw it, and he wasn't afraid to tell me so. He actually called me a "prick" in practice one day, and I absolutely knew the reason. As the football season continued, we pushed each other to be better players. I gained respect for him on the field, but I didn't know if we had a chance to get along off the field. So I kept my distance. What Rich didn't know was I'd had a past experience with a high school teammate that played tight end and that experience would play a major role in our friendship.

I was in the sixth grade, and I had caught the bus to school. My older siblings had caught the same bus with the same bus driver for two consecutive years prior. When I stepped on the bus for the first time, the driver knew who I was, and she allowed me to bend the bus rules a little. There was a kid on the bus the other kids called JP. He was the "popular kid" with the girls and the athletes, playing in the local neighborhood sports leagues. JP was a big kid for his age. For some reason, he and I didn't get along, and we fought a lot. Looking back, our fights were only child's play at first, but it got serious over time before it got better.

I hadn't experienced my young growth spurt yet, so I was still on the small side of life. JP didn't scare or intimidate me, and I stood up to him every time. I remembered my uncles telling me not to pick a fight with someone smaller than me unless they started it, and even if they started it, I should be patient. But when it came to someone bigger than me, my uncles told me and taught me how to go after him with everything I had and to bring the devil with me. And my uncles taught me, specifically, how to do that.

JP and I fought off-and-on for two years and then in eighth grade, it stopped. I tried out for football and made the team in junior high. I thought we were going to be enemies for a long time, but we slowly became good friends by the time I was a senior in high school.

My relationship with Rich didn't start out the same as my high school teammate. However, my past experience taught me not to hold a grudge, find patience, and avoid judging him if he didn't like me at first. I could have taken the easy road and thought it was because of my race, but I didn't. I understood that Rich and I were competing in practice. I was not his enemy on or off the practice field, and deep down inside, I hoped he understood that, too. I missed the opportunity to get to know him off the field before we became roommates, but when I became his roommate, the opportunity stared at me in the face.

I learned Rich had been exposed to all types of kids growing up because he played three different sports (football, basketball, and lacrosse) as a kid. His teammates came from all walks of life in the Charlottesville area. Rich invited friends to his home to play football in his front yard, and more than half were Black. It was a life lesson he would carry for a long time. Rich was from a middle-class family, even though his father was a college coach (some coaches weren't making enormous amounts of money in the '70s and early '80s).

I had, without a doubt, a different view of Perry when I first noticed him during preseason camp. I thought he was from a privileged, affluent, entitled class, with his White power structure to lean on and nothing to worry about. I assumed that because of his classy all-American good looks, preppy clothes, and his hot rod, red sports car. I didn't find out where he was from until the second week of training camp. Perry's personality was the example of the perfect Southern gentleman. His attitude was great, and he always had a smile on his face (something else we had in common). I was sure Perry came from a higher economic class than Rich and me, but he didn't wear it on his sleeve or rub it in our faces. He wasn't obnoxious, spoiled, or act as if everything was handed to him. Well, almost everything.

Perry dressed in Polo shirts and Tommy "everything" Hilfiger. From what I could see, it was only the top brands for Perry. Perry has also been exposed to kids from different backgrounds while growing up playing sports. From the time he was six, he played on football teams with Black kids. The ratio was balanced Black and White, and he learned to treat his teammates and competitors equally and judge them on their merits and not on preconceived notions or stereotypes.

As word began to spread about me being homeless and crashing in my teammates' room, I was a little worried. I wasn't worried about myself. I was worried about my roommates getting in trouble because of me. I was worried about being "flushed out" to our coaches by one of my Black or White teammates living in our dorm, a teammate looking to elevate his standing as a player with a coach. Or would it be one of my White dormmates, a guy referred to as "Chuck" by the athletes and friends (cool dudes) of Black athletes in the dorm.

A fellow student, whose sole purpose it would seem, was to dime out or point out to the university every potential school infraction committed by an athlete. But it never happened and by the time I was totally relaxed and okay with my living situation, I didn't care what anyone said, and I didn't give a ham-sandwich what anyone thought about me being homeless.

It didn't matter to me what anyone said about me being homeless because what really mattered was that I had people on campus and teammates willing to help. I knew some of my classmates and teammates questioned why Rich and Perry were helping me. But there was no Black-lash or White-lash toward my new roommates for helping me through my homeless condition. To my knowledge, none of my White teammates called my roommates names or referred to them openly as the "N_lover" or used any dog whistles or racial slurs in their conversations. None of my Black teammates asked me what it was like to share a room with two "red necks," "hicks," "hillbillies," White boys or referred to them using other derogatory names for Whites. My goal was to protect my roommates from any grief.

Rich and Perry had something in their hearts to help a teammate out. It was as if the dreams of so many were happening at the right time. As the word began to spread around campus to and from more athletes about me being homeless, some athletes saw me as a hopeless case and others understood what I was going through. I was no different than most athletes: passionate, emotional, and sometimes, very opinionated. Most, if not all, football players are naturally emotional and aggressive (it's part of our make-up) and most basketball players are passive-aggressive and sell more Wolf tickets then they intend to use. I learned this from being around them a lot.

Only a few of my teammates and other athletes (basketball players) joked around with me about being homeless. They would say things, such as, "How you doing nomad?" or "Where you been, gypsy?" or "What's up, hobo?" It was all in good fun, but at the risk of sounding arrogant or cocky. Being known around campus as a tough guy or hard-nosed football player on the field pretty much limited how many guys would say anything to my face without being absolutely positive we were friends. Because they would end up having a bad day with the sons of the South.

TOPIC 34. FAMILY RACE

I spent days and nights with my roommates talking and getting to know more about them off the field. We were three sons of the South trying to make our way in Yankee country. I noticed my roommates were very comfortable with all my Black teammates, and I picked up from our conversations that their comfort started with their parents. Rich was born in Richmond and was the oldest of three with two younger sisters, Analisa and Ginger. They were all two years apart. His father, Dick Lage, coached football at the University of Virginia, and his mother, Emily, was a teacher. Mr. Lage left a legacy for his son to follow. Rich was exposed to college athletes from all walks of life. His father hosted players of different races and backgrounds at his home for barbeques and clambakes. From an early age, Rich had been exposed to athletes on the college level from all races, and he had watched them build good relationships with each other. So I quickly learned why Rich was a top hand.

Rich's dad was a college All-American football player at Lenoir-Rhyne College in the early 60s. His dad understood the foundation of sports: the importance of acceptance, teamwork, family, communication, and relationships. His mother had taught Rich life lessons regarding race and class. Rich attended public schools. His mom wouldn't pick him up from school after practice. She made him catch the activity bus home after practice for all three sports. He was able to ride the bus with kids from all backgrounds and that enabled him to develop an organic friendship with many kids (Black and White). He traveled to different communities and saw the homes of his teammates and friends. He learned that not every kid came from the same economic background.

Perry was born in Savannah, Georgia and grew up in Bluffton and Hilton Head, South Carolina. Perry was the older of two boys. His brother, Chris, was three years younger. His father, Frank, worked for the local township as a building inspector, and Perry's mom, Patsy, made sure her sons understood that everyone was created equal in

God's eyes. Perry didn't grow up in a blended community, so his parents hoped he would receive his exposure through his love of sports. Perry participated in sports from the time he was able to physically play. Perry's dad graduated from University of South Carolina. He was a Gamecock and was a big fan of sports. Perry's parents believed in the power of education, and he attended a small, private prep school from kindergarten until he graduated from high school. He started working at age eleven at the local grocery store and later worked at the local golf course near his home. Perry learned a lot from working at the golf club. His job duties included cleaning clubs, shining shoes, working the driving range, and basically catering to the members, and that's where he developed more relationships with people of color. He learned a lot about life during those times.

My conversations with Rich and Perry were open and honest. Our conversations revealed we had a lot in common, and I was more surprised of that than they were. Sure, we were athletes who loved sports, but I discovered they loved their families just as much as I did. We talked about our siblings, our parents, and other family members. Rich and I talked about our sisters all the time, and we loved hearing the stories Perry told us about his little brother. Through story, Chris slowly became the younger brother Rich and I never had. Perry and I stayed away from talking about our fathers when Rich was around. I think it was a learning experience for both of us. I told Perry my dad was involved in music and had a band in his younger days. And when the three of us talked about our mothers, that's when the earth would shake. Rich, Perry, and I loved our mothers more than we loved football, and we figured at least two of us were definitely mama's boys.

Rich, Perry, and I were quickly becoming more than teammates. We were developing a special relationship and a bond. We were becoming brothers, and I realized how easy it was to do. We had a foundation to lean on as roommates, the foundation of trust in your teammates. In order for me to fully embrace my roommates, I, as a Black kid, had to set aside all the stereotypes I had heard growing up about Whites and trust what I experienced during my time at 'Nova. I had to give my roommates every chance to become my brothers and family just as I had given my Black teammates.

Our first two games were away games, which made our third game our first home game of the season. I didn't meet Perry's parents during the first two away games because I didn't travel with the team. His parents attended every game. Perry's parents planned to stop by our room after our first home game before heading back to South Carolina. Perry met his parents in the tunnel of the stadium. I was the last player to leave the locker room because I wanted to spend some time alone before heading back to the room. My jersey was clean because I barely broke a sweat standing on the sidelines in the heat. Waiting outside the locker in the tunnel was Roxanne, the classmate I had helped on the first day of school. She came to the game (she said to see me play), and it took me by surprise. I was surprised because I told her—when we first met—that I didn't play much, but I guess it didn't matter. We talked for a few minutes as I walked her to the SEPTA train stop, and then she headed home (she lived a few train stops from campus).

My mood changed after running into Roxanne and my focus turned toward meeting Perry's parents. I didn't want to disappoint Perry by being late to meet his parents, so I hustled to the dorm and made it in time to meet his family. During my previous conversation with Perry, he painted a beautiful picture of his parents, but I was concerned that his parents wouldn't accept me because of my race. I was old enough to know that you never know what's in someone's heart until you meet them, look them in the eyes, and see their reaction. I had a strong argument, as a Black kid from the South, to be a little skeptical, but Perry's family deserved the same level of respect and opportunity I had given my Black teammates' parents.

My thoughts or feelings of doubt and defensive reservations were a waste of time. Perry's description of his parents was spot-on. His mother was the beautiful Southern bell with an infectious personality, and his dad was kind, sociable, and basically, a tall teddy bear. His parents were sympathetic and very supportive of me sharing the room with their son. They invited Rich and me to their home to go fishing, and I felt like they truly meant it. So Rich and I started to make plans to take them up on the offer. After I met Perry's parents, it solidified my feelings that we were on our way to becoming more than teammates.

A few nights later, we settled into our routines and busy schedules as athletes. I knew Perry looked to Rich and me to guide him through his new life as a freshman and a newcomer to living with roommates. Perry grew up having his own room, and Rich did as well. I, on the other hand, had shared a room with my brother. So I completely understood how not wanting your sibling (or a roommate) to invade your personal space within a 10x15 box. It's a wonderful dream but unrealistic and not likely possible in a dorm room. Perry, being the youngest in our room, was very impressionable and inquisitive. If he didn't know something, he would ask. It took me some time at 'Nova to get accustomed to Whites asking me personal questions. I grew up in a culture of "mind your own business," but by the time Perry came along, I was over it. I finally understood that some of my White classmates genuinely wanted to get to know me and learn a few personal things about me.

TOPIC 35. TEAMMATES RACE

I felt more comfortable talking to my roommates about sports, specifically football. As athletes, we talked *X*s and *O*s almost every day, but we also passed the time by talking about our pasts regarding sports. We'd share real-life stories and experiences from our youth, and those conversations evolved into deeper conversations. We talked about when we started playing sports and what our experiences were like. Rich was born a gym rat, and Perry was an outdoor kid.

My roommates' parents gave them a gift that would travel with them to college. My roommates played sports with kids from all walks of life. Their teammates crossed racial lines, religious lines, socioeconomic lines, and more than likely, political lines. Their experience of traveling as a team to compete against teams across district lines, city lines, and state lines was a positive experience, as was going through practice drills and winning and losing games together. Hearing the crowd screaming and cheering for them as a multicultural youth group was unforgettable. Routinely hearing the words family, team, blood, sweat, and tears . . . they were ingrained in these guys.

I had no exposure to playing organized sports at an early age with Black or White kids. Sure, I played football in the street or in someone's front yard with the kids in my neighborhood, but that was it. I didn't participate in little league, Pee Wee/Pop Warner, or recreational sports. My earliest memory of wanting to play organized football was when I watched football on TV. And I wasn't as lucky as the kids in my neighborhood or school because my mom wouldn't allow me to play. She told me I was never going to play football, and I didn't know why. My brother was one year older, and he could play whatever sport he wanted. I remember my brother staying after school in elementary school to try out for the basketball team. So the next day, I decided to do the same. I stayed after school to try out for the basketball team.

I was in the warm-up line when my mom showed up. She walked from our house to the school and pulled me off the court. The coach didn't know who she was, and he yelled out, "Lady, lady, what are you doing?"

My mom turned to the coach and said, as she pointed to my brother, "He can play, but this one is coming home with me." I turned to see what the coach would do next, but I knew from the look on his face, my mom had given him the "don't mess with me protective look." I was very familiar with that look. That's the look Black women in my family give when they mean business. I didn't know what the word embarrassed meant at that age, but I knew what the word felt like. I asked my mom while we were walking back home why I couldn't try out for the team.

She said, "You're my baby boy, and I don't want you to play." And just before the next words spilled out of my mouth, the "why" or "but you let" I caught myself because I was not ready for what would've come next, the consequence of questioning her, so we didn't talk about it for a long time.

Perry eventually asked me how and when I started playing football. "It was my uncle," I told him. For years, I had begged and bugged Uncle Joe to talk to my mom about letting me play football, and he kept telling me he would try. My aunts discussed the topic around the dinner table at my grandmother's house on Sundays, but that's about as far as it went. Until one day during the summer, just before I started junior high, my uncle came over to the house to drop off some ice cream. I ate a lot of ice cream, hoping it would help me gain weight. He asked me if I was ready to play football. I told him I was. My uncle was the younger of my mom's two brothers. I guess he understood how I felt.

My uncle waited until my mom returned home from work and that's when all heck broke loose. He immediately got into her face, asking her when she was going to let me play football. It turned into a shouting match, one that almost came to blows. My uncle was willing to fight his older sister so I could play. He understood how much I wanted to play, and he knew how much I loved football. He believed I could learn to play the game and would work hard to make the team in junior high . . . or maybe he just got tired of me asking him to talk to my mom.

I remember the first laughable moment my roommates and I had together. Rich and I got tired of coming back to the room and finding Perry's clothes thrown all over the place, even under his bed. We couldn't go the entire semester dealing with that. Rich and I decided we were going to teach Perry how to wash his clothes and put them away, or we were going to kill him by the end of the semester.

During training camp, I had heard a few of the guys in the locker room talking about walking into Rich and Perry's room and finding a mess. I had passed by their room a few times during camp and noticed Perry's clothes on the floor or stacked in the corner of his room. He wasn't a trifling mess; he just needed a little coaching on how to wash his dirty clothes and put them away.

One night after class, I walked into the room and his clothes were all over the place. I had had enough! I said, "Perry, you're killing me with these clothes all over the place."

"What do you want me to do with them?" he said.

"I don't give a ham-sandwich where you put them, just not everywhere," I told him.

Rich asked him if he knew how to wash his clothes.

Perry replied "No."

So I helped him separate his clean clothes from the dirty ones. Rich and I taught Perry how to use laundry detergent and how to separate his whites from his dark clothes. As Rich finished the demo, I chimed in to lighten the mood and said, "Whites and darks should only be separated when washing clothes, not with people."

Perry looked at me and replied, "You're not going anywhere, brother."

I gave Perry credit; he handled it very well. In the end, Perry got the last laugh. He found a full-service laundry and dry-cleaning business on the Main Line to wash, fold, and place his clothes in a box for pickup. After that experience, the three of us were in our Southern race as roommates and teammates. Basically, we were a social experiment with the weighty potential of either passing or failing.

Rich and Perry had established their relationship during Perry's recruiting visit. When Perry made his decision to come to 'Nova, he called Rich and gave him the good news. Rich was excited. Perry asked Rich to think about rooming together because their relationship had started on a positive note. Rich agreed and told Perry, "Southerners gotta stick together." Perry wanted to bring his car to 'Nova, and Rich was more than happy to help him get it registered on campus.

Perry was someone with whom it was very easy to start and hold a conversation with. One night, after a long day of classes, football practice, class again, and study hall, we were relaxing in our room and Perry seemed very interested in how I made it to 'Nova. I was more than happy to tell him my story.

First, I told him, I started my college career at Cheyney, and then transferred to 'Nova. He had never heard of Cheyney, so I explained the difference between Cheyney and Villanova. I confessed to Perry that I was gullible for not looking deeper into the school when I had the chance. He wanted to know why. I told him I had the chance to research 'Nova before I transferred, and I didn't. I also explained that my sister told me I was wrong about the racial make-up of the university, but I wouldn't listen to her. He wanted to know if I experienced culture shock when I arrived at Vanilla-nova. I didn't because I was taught never to be afraid of any situation, anything, or anybody. And with three years at 'Nova under my belt, I had learned the world was bigger than I could've ever imagined.

I told him, "On the outside, each university appears Black and White, but it's deeper than that." I spoke about the similarities and the differences, such as students being competitive academically, socially, and personally; the peer pressure at both was real; and the need to be accepted filtered through both campuses. I added, "'Nova parties more than Cheyney." I finished with how both schools encouraged ideas and hopes for students' futures and how both campuses prepared students for the American dream.

Perry had opened the door for me to take interest in his background because he was interested in mine. Initially, Perry and I were the most talkative in the group of three. We completely understood that Rich was still working his way through the loss of his father.

CHAPTER VI

Conversation Race

TOPIC 36. HAIR RACE

I was able to build a relationship with my roommates that I didn't expect. One night, I returned to our room after my night class, and my roommates were watching TV. We talked and watched TV for a while, and then it was time for me to get a shower. I quickly jumped into the shower and returned to the room to finish up. Perry noticed me going through my pre-bed routine. I started with rubbing lotions all over my body and putting a hair product in my hair, brushing it, and then placing my doo-rag/dew-rag (some call it a wave cap) on my head. Perry asked me what I was doing. I told him I was getting ready for bed. He seemed amazed and a little bewildered with all the things I did before I called it a night. From where I stood, Perry had no preconceived opinion or misconception about any part of my routine. He simply asked me why I

159

put so much lotion on, what it was I had put in my hair, and what I had put on my head.

I'll never forget the look Rich had on his face. I could only guess what Rich was thinking at that moment. I knew, with his background, Rich had a deeper experience being around Black athletes on a college level, so I took the time to describe to Perry my bedtime routine and why I had it.

First, I started with the lotion. I described to him one of the downfalls or side effects of coming from the South to the North for me was developing very dry skin and the lotion helped me to keep my skin smooth, soft, and not ashy. I told him the lotion acted as a moisturizer after I finished my shower. I told him brothers and sisters don't like ashy skin.

Rich chimed in and said, with his dry sense of humor, "You got that right, brother."

"Not all Black people are the same shade, tone, or complexion." I wasn't being mean or condescending, and Perry understood that. I continued with, "Some Blacks use more lotion than others, but one thing is certain, we use a product of some type to keep our skin looking good. It doesn't matter if you're dark, brown, or have light skin; it's embarrassing to walk out any door and in public with ashy skin. And if you're not wearing cologne, then cocoa butter lotion is the next best thing. I made a point of telling him, as a Black man looking at a White person, I can't immediately tell if you need lotion or not." I gave him some advice, if he cared about his appearance, he should use lotion every day because of the drier air up north, especially in the winter."

Now it was time to discuss my hair. I thought for a second whether I should get into the conversation about hair. I had two choices: brush him off or give our new developing friendship the respect it deserved. And I knew as an athlete and a QB, the pressure of being uncomfortable was something he could handle, so I continued. I was careful not to come off as a militant, hostile, or defensive about his question. I wanted to be as positive and animated as I could because when it comes to most Black people and our hair, it gets "real" personal.

I started with the easy part before getting into the more complex descriptions and explanations. I restated that not all Black people are the same. Not all Black people have the same type of hair. Some have thick hair, others have curly hair, and still others have wavy hair (there's a difference). Some have short hair and some have a head full of hair. My hair was thin and a little curly but without a doubt, my hair was not nappy. I told him don't ever refer to a Black person's hair (if you're not friends) as nappy. Those are fightin' words.

I continued to explain to Perry that I got my hair cut based on the style I liked and the type of fresh cut that suited my head. Perry was smart and sharp enough to notice the different hairstyles the brothers on the team sported. There were multiple popular hairstyles the brothers liked. They sported everything from a low-cut fade to a high-top fade, a box fade, medium to low Afros, and one or two of our biracial brothers had hair they styled or cut in many different styles. I asked him to think about our White teammates and how many different hairstyles are sported.

The product portion of the conversation was next. I used the hair product, in part, to help style my hair the way I liked. I was sure Perry hadn't heard of the product, and that was okay. I explained there were hair product commercials all over TV for White folks. However, in order to see any Black products on mainstream TV, a White person would need to carve out their entire day and sit in front of multiple TV sets on all the major and secondary networks to find one Black hair product commercial. Then I said, the brothers don't have as many choices as Whites, and he totally got it. I showed Perry the product I used and then demonstrated how I applied it. I followed with, "Not all the brothers on the team use the same product for their hair."

Now my brush was as important as his brush or comb. My brush helped me style my hair the way I wanted it to look. He could clearly see the waves in my hair and in order to keep my hair looking nice and tight, I had to meticulously brush my hair because during the football season, putting on and taking off my football helmet, laying on the bench to lift weights, and the routine of taking a shower in the morning after practice and before bed, messed up my hairstyle. That's why I carried my brush in my bookbag and some carry their brushes in their back pockets. I finished this part of our conversation with, "When my low-cut, wavy fade doesn't look nice and tight, I'm not happy." Perry laughed and Rich chimed in again, and said, "Brothers act like it's the end of the world if their hair ain't right," and I said, "He's right," as I smiled.

I finished this part of the conversation with the last and most important part of my routine. The doo-rag. My doo-rag was made of nylon material, and I tied it on my head to keep my hair in place during the night because I dream a lot when I sleep, so I toss and turn. I put it on my head so my hair product wouldn't get all over the pillow or the end of my red futon. We ended our discussion with me advising Perry that if he got the chance to see X-man cutting a few guys' hair, to do it . . . "Check it out, and you'll learn something." Our teammate, X-man, cut hair to make a couple of dollars here and there. Our conversation was very close to a locker room or barbershop conversation. I was able to recognize through our conversations that Perry's exposure to Black culture was different than Rich's, and that was okay. But what I absolutely knew was that I had less exposure to Whites growing up than each of my roommates had experienced with Blacks.

One night, the subject of the Catholic Church service came up. During home games, the team would attend Mass on campus in the St. Thomas of Villanova Church. We discussed the university requirement that all students were required to take two religion courses before their junior year and free to take any electives of our choice after fulfilling that requirement. Rich hilariously referred to himself as a left-handed Catholic. I didn't feel attending a Catholic university with my Baptist background was a major adjustment. I looked at it as a learning experience, and I quickly learned the differences between the Baptist and Catholic religions. I learned a few of my Black teammates were Catholic. I had no idea, and I assumed most, if not all of my Black teammates and classmates were like me, in the Baptist denomination, but I was wrong.

From the time I arrived at 'Nova, I had heard stories about the nuns in Catholic schools. The nuns were very demanding and discipline-oriented, and that didn't weird me out because my grandmother was the head usher for our church and there were a few similarities. When you're related to any ranking member of a Black church and everyone knows it, it was very difficult to get away with anything as a kid. And behaving badly was not the word used in our Black church. It was "mind your *p*s and *q*s" or else (meaning—pay attention, be quiet, and no horsing around or you're going to get it) while the pastor is preaching and during the entire service. My grandmother's church was a relatively small church compared to most Southern Black churches.

I caught the church bus with my siblings every Sunday morning. If we missed the bus, then my mom drove us, and that meant we missed the Sunday school class, but we'd make it in time for church service. In the Black community, you don't go to church "kicking and screaming" because that would be a recipe for disaster. Looking back on my young church experiences, as a good friend would call it, we were forced to visit God every Sunday. I was not familiar with the Catholic, Lutheran, or Episcopal churches growing up. I only knew one person outside the Baptist religion, and it was my aunt, who was a Jehovah's Witness.

I ended my part of the conversation telling Rich and Perry about my first Catholic service on campus. I had been a little nervous because I had never been to a Catholic service. Once it was over, I thought, "Man that wasn't hard." It was easy, over, and done within no time. "I could do this again. It was only an hour service." My grandmother's church and most Black Southern Baptist church services were two or three hours long and that's not including Sunday school. You've got the preacher preaching, the choir singing many hymns, deacon readings, announcements, baptisms, and don't forget the offerings. Other teammates that I shared my church experience with couldn't believe how long our church services lasted.

TOPIC 37. STEREOTYPES RACE

Without a meal card, it was a little difficult to manage eating, but it wasn't the end of my world. I managed my work-study funds well and with help from Mr. D., Rich, and Perry, I didn't miss a meal. I had worried about where my next meal would come from in the past but not during my homeless hardship. Mr. D. treated me to breakfast or lunch more than a few times. Rich and Perry would bring food back to the room, whether I needed it or not, for the entire year. I often had a late class, and by the time I returned to the room, there was food available. On a few occasions, if my roommates had other plans for dinner, they'd leave me their meal cards.

Rich, Perry, and I talked about any and everything. We were young, but we pushed through every cultural, social, and stereotypical issue that many people would be uncomfortable to try. We discussed food, movies, music, politics, and more.

Each of us was a meat lover, and we talked about growing up eating different types of food prepared by our family members (mom's, grandmother's, aunt's, or close friends of the family). We shared stories about a family member who developed a reputation of cooking something yummy, delicious, tasty, and outstanding or as we would say down South, she or he "put their foot in it." My mom was the best at cooking fried pork chops (crispy on the outside and tender on the inside, like chicken.) I loved those pork chops, and I dreamed about them while I was away from home. I shared with my roommates how I discovered the Italian family's passion for cooking and how Black families' passion for cooking was the same. For both, it's a very important part of the family experience. Everyone worked together to bring a positive family experience. The kitchen was the arena that brought joy to the family unit.

During one food-related conversation, Rich, Perry, and I discovered something about each other we didn't previously know. We all loved fried chicken. When I learned that my roommates enjoyed fried chicken as much as I did, it became our Sunday dinner routine. It started during the football season, on Sundays after our team meetings. Rich, Perry, and I relaxed in our dorm room watching NFL games or golf. And later that night, we jumped into Perry's car, tap Mac/ATM, and headed to our favorite fried chicken spot for takeout. Over time, teammates with cars or who had access to cars took food orders and joined us on our ride to City Line Avenue. We returned to the dorm with "chicken, chicken, and more chicken. Chicken with red beans and rice, biscuits, coleslaw, and more." The smell of our chicken meals flowed through the halls and guys would come out of their rooms to comment on how great our food smelled. I knew which White guys grew up eating Popeyes's Chicken or Church's Chicken because they'd tell me.

I learned what type of chicken meals White families enjoyed. Everyone was different, based on the region of the country they were from and their family background. I'd seen my White teammates, classmates, and the Main Line community eat chicken prepared in different ways. Our food services on campus prepared all types of chicken meals, and the majority of my White classmates ate those meals and enjoyed them. My White classmates enjoyed chicken as a casserole, fried, baked, cordon bleu, and more. I loved the "wing dings" from a small Main Line town called Wayne, and I had to have pickles (I didn't have to wait to get fried pickles served in the South) with my chicken, or it wasn't a complete meal.

During one of our conversations about Black culture, one of my Black teammates, Rashid Walker from New York, said, "Blacks don't own all the chicken restaurants or win all the chicken wing eating contests."

"What a great comeback if I needed to repeat it," I thought. I came to believe that racists (when given the opportunity to show their true colors of hate) fell back to what they believed would insult a Black person or get an emotional outburst or hurt a Black person's feelings by repeating the racial slur, "All Black people eat fried chicken." After hearing this stereotype repeated a few times, getting angry, and maybe wanting to fight, it was time to use my head. By the time my teammates, guys on our floor, and others enjoyed our Sunday routine and special event, my emotions and thoughts evolved to: "All fair and good-hearted White folks should get upset and insulted by that racist comment because they love chicken too."

Another group activity we enjoyed together, which helped bring us closer as roommates and teammates, involved watching soap operas. Our crew (Rich, Perry, JD, X, and others) loved watching soaps. We talked about them, joked about them, and bragged about doing it. A group of Black and White football athletes watching soap operas was something our classmates didn't believe, and our girlfriends found it very interesting. If we didn't have class during our shows, you could catch us watching the soaps to relax before practice, and it hurt a little if we missed one episode. We came up with new show titles for the top two shows we watched, "The Young and the Restless" and "The Bold and the Beautiful." We renamed the "Young and the Restless," the "Stupid and the Foolish," and the "Bold and the Beautiful" was renamed the "Skeezers and the Tramps."

Our girlfriends watched with us and girls who wanted to be our girlfriends (we discovered later) watched in JD and X-man's room. I believe watching soaps helped our relationships with our girlfriends. Hear me out. I think it nixed one of the macho stereotypes about football players. They found it unbelievable and later, it became amusing to watch us get emotionally involved. Word began to spread inside a few of the female dorms and around campus. We kept our room doors open, sometimes, because the room was so crowded during the shows, we needed the hallway space. When visiting classmates or guys living down the hall walked pass our rooms, we'd hush or shush them if they were talking.

We got a kick and a laugh out of watching their faces as we yelled at them to keep the noise down so we could hear our shows. We talked about the characters just as much as the ladies did, and we didn't care if everyone in our dorm or on campus knew. And as for our crew, there was no reason to care what anyone thought. We'd say to our girlfriends, or to any female or to any dude with that look of astonishment on their faces after finding out we watched soaps, "There's no shame in our game." Besides, what male classmate, no matter his size (big or small), would be foolish enough to say something or tease a group of football players for watching soaps? No way! It never happened, and if they did, their comments would not have been good for their health.

I don't remember how the subject came up or how it started, it just happened while we were hanging out passing time one night. The topic of movies we'd seen as kids or loved as teenagers got everyone excited. Participating in the conversation were Rich, Perry, JD, X-Man, Bobby, and Rashid. The movies starring Bruce Lee were the most entertaining. We helped each other remember the names of characters in the movie. We recalled the friends or family members we were with when we watched them. It seemed like every kid in my neighborhood and my high school loved Bruce Lee. After our conversation that night, I learned my White teammates and their friends loved Bruce Lee the same as my Black teammates. We agreed that seeing grown Black men and White men act as if they were Bruce Lee, the martial arts hero, was quite entertaining as kids.

We talked about how horror movies always killed off the Black people first. My Black teammates added their "two cents" in the discussion, but I was surprised to find out my White roommates noticed and agreed with us. The cat was out of the bag. We weren't being overly sensitive about it. Ideas were exchanged about what we would do and how we would escape if we were in that horror movie situation. All of us weighed in, describing how we would react to the scary event in the moment. Everyone agreed we'd do the total opposite of what the Black person in the movie scene did. We understood it was just a movie, but what we did agree on was all of the scary movies in the '70s and '80s had one token Black person in it, and the reason seemed obvious: to be killed very early on in the movie. I was impressed with the fact that my roommates noticed it, and my Black teammates in the room noticed, too.

Then, someone opened his mouth and brought up the movie, *Roots*. "Oh, snap! Let's see how this goes," I thought. Alex Haley's late '70s miniseries about slaves in America was reported to have been watched by most Americans. Rich and Perry remembered watching it, too. Everyone in the room at some point and time had watched the movie growing up. We talked about some of the characters—Kunta-Kinte, the Mandinka warrior played by LeVar Burton, Fiddler, played by Lou Gossett, Jr., Chicken George, and others. We talked about parts in the miniseries that were etched in our memories: when slaves got married, how they jumped over a broom, and how many different ways the slaves tried to survive. We didn't need to discuss how horrible slaves were treated. Rich and Perry didn't have to say much or try to overdo it by saying how bad things were for the slaves. They listened and laughed with us and went through the emotional roller coaster ride with us. Talking about *Roots* in our own way was a history lesson for all of us. We didn't point fingers or try to make Rich and Perry feel bad or embarrass them about what happened to the slaves. I gained respect from all of my teammates, Black and White, in the room during and after our conversation because of the way we handled the conversation. Talking about the miniseries became a shared experience between my Black and White teammates. I was surprised to find out that *Roots* had the impact it did on my roommates.

We shifted from the *Roots* conversation to politics in America. I was blessed to be surrounded by some of the smartest brothers, Black and

White, in my life. I remember my mother and a few of my high school teachers telling me, "You're better off hanging around smart people. You might learn something because you don't want to be known for hanging out with people going nowhere." My teammate, Rashid, was quietly known as the militant brother of the group. His mom was a teacher, and he was highly intelligent. He majored in economics, and he understood the positive, as well as the deep underbelly, of American business. Rich and Bobby majored in marketing, Jeff majored in finance, and Perry and X-man were business majors.

Ronald Reagan was in his second term as president and his trickle-down economics plan wasn't going well for everyone in the country. My teammates were talking about bigger or smaller government, spending, lower taxes, more or less regulations, and what it truly meant to them. And it was well over my head, but I listened.

Then Rev. Jesse Jackson and Rev. Al Sharpton blow up the conversation. Everyone supported Rev. Jackson running for president, and I did as well, but my gut told me that he was a selfish person only out for himself, the type of man that would smile in your face while stabbing you in the back. I was one of the few who supported Rev. Al. I liked him because, in my mind and heart, he was the type of guy who loved fighting bullies. And everyone who knew me found out, I loved fighting bullies.

For as long as I can remember, music has always played a role in athletics. I listened to music before, during, and after my workouts. When I wasn't mentally focused or physically ready to work out, I used music to psych myself up to start and finish my workout routine. Music inspired me to give more when I thought I had no energy left in my tank. My goal was to go all out and push myself to the limit. Music didn't make my workouts any easier, but it helped me stay in the right frame of mind and made the time go by faster. Music triggered and provided the jolt of energy I needed to enjoy my painful workouts.

Rich, Perry, and I talked about the different types of music we liked. We agreed that jazz, R&B, pop, and rock produced great music. I surprised them when they found out that I liked country music, too. They learned that I loved all types of music. "Have you heard of or remember the Commodores and their song, "Brick House?" I asked them. And they did. I told them that my aunt, Rosylin, won the Ms. Brick House contest, a talent show/beauty contest promoted by our local radio station, back in the day. The Commodores were in town for their concert tour, and she got the chance to meet them. They were truly impressed.

In the '80s, rap music was under attack; it was being described as dangerous from a number of groups (politicians, civic leaders, religious leaders, media, a small number of Blacks, and a larger number of Whites). However, a small group of Whites did embrace rap music in the '80s. I witnessed Whites around campus accept rap music and join the rap movement. I remember a few of my Black teammates encouraging my roommates to learn the lyrics to rap songs they liked, and they did. It turned out to be one of the experiences we used to build better relationships.

One day, X-man came walking down the hall, yelling at the top of his lungs, "I got it and it's hot. Meeting in my room." His parents were executives in the music industry, and he had gotten his hands on the soon-to-be-released *Heart Break* album by New Edition on cassette tape. Johnny Gill was the new member of the group. As our crew finished classes and made our way back to the dorm, one by one we stopped by JD and X's room because the music was playing. We couldn't stop listening or talking about how much we loved every song on the album. The music played for days and days, almost twenty-four hours a day. There were so many of us—a few in JD and X's room, and the rest hung out in the hall. The music fused into our bones, it was time to take our shared love of the music and the album to a new level.

We had heard the songs so many times that we knew it was time to sing each and every word on the cassette tape together. As each member of our crew entered the floor, they joined in the singing and entertainment for others to see.

When Rich (now a.k.a. "Big Country') entered, he began singing and dancing with his brothers. He didn't know every word, and he didn't hit every note, but not all the brothers did either. Rich built a good relationship with anyone who wanted to build a relationship with him, and my crew of brothers gave him the respect he had earned and deserved. We didn't fit into any stereotypes to him, and he didn't fit into any stereotypes to us . . . because we were family.

TOPIC 38. NICKNAME RACE

One deep social and cultural tradition of the South, regardless if you were born Black or White, is receiving a nickname. I always found it interesting how or why people received their nicknames. In the South, people are bestowed a nickname for all types of reasons (good or bad), and it doesn't matter if the name was well thought out or not. But, if the name stuck, one would hope it was for a good reason. Some Southern nicknames are strange, others funny, and some ethnic, based on appearance or family relations. I grew up knowing people with nicknames, such as Mosquito, Bones, Yogi, Billy Boy, Lady Bird, Tiny, Slim, Froggy, Lemon-Drop, and more. Earning a nickname in sports is common on every team and in every community, park, venue, and state in our great union. Athletic nicknames can be authentic, colorful, entertaining, charming, descriptive, and enduring, and having one can be an honor or a curse. Some athletes bring their nicknames to the sport they play, and others receive a name because of their accomplishments in the sport they play.

One of the greatest athletes with the biggest nicknames and the biggest personalities was Charles Barkley (The Round Mound of Rebound). One day, Perry was heading to the King of Prussia Mall to pick up some new and very expensive clothes, and he asked me to tag along. After we arrived at the mall, we ran into Charles. I introduced Perry to him. Charles could tell Perry was from the South and asked him where he was from. We had a short but great conversation. And Charles gained a new fan. Although my roommates and I were Southerners to our core, not all of us had a nickname.

Perry arrived on campus without a nickname, and if he had a nickname, he decided not to let it travel with him. I tried several names for Perry. "Big Head" was one but nothing stuck, so it was up to his class group to award him a name he'd keep for life before he graduated. Rich was saddled with the nickname "Big County" by roommates Jeff and Xavier. I wasn't surprised that X-man was involved because he was from the Dirty South. Rich earned his nickname because of his strong Southern accent, love of country music, calm personality, and big and tall body frame. X-man gave Rich his nickname as a term of endearment. Rich was known as one of the coolest—along with Bob Brady (a.k.a. White Chocolate)—White dudes on the team.

One night, I received a call on the hall phone, and the person who took the call knocked on our room door with a confused look on his face. He looked at the room number to make sure he had the correct room. The call was for me, but the caller had used the name on my government birth certificate. He was confused because my mom had asked for me by the name that she and my dad decided suited me. When he asked my mom to repeat it, she remembered that not all of my classmates knew my birth name. Perry was also stunned and confused when he heard my name because he had no idea what my legal name was. Perry didn't have the time on the field, the shared experiences, or the memories from the previous season. Perry thought my legal name was Bo-Dean and my nickname was "The Hammer," based on what he had heard during preseason practice. Our starting QB, Kurt Shultz, was the first teammate to call me "The Hammer" during the previous season. Kurt would lead the chant with a few of my teammates during warm-ups: "Bring out the wood 'cause here comes The Hammer." Coach Johnson, the wide receiver coach, and Coach John Burke, the special team's coach, agreed.

After I spoke to my mom, I returned to our room and shared my full story. My best friend in the neighborhood where I grew up, Jesse-Duke Walker, had given me my nickname, Bo-Dean. Jesse was born in Bronx, New York and moved to Virginia, then to Florida. We met in junior high school. Jesse, from time to time, came to watch me during football practice and attended my games. Jesse liked football, but he was a city kid, and playing football wasn't his thing. At the end of my junior high football season, a few of my teammates and I were picked by the coaches to move up and practice with the high school team for a few weeks, which was a huge accomplishment for me. I was over the moon excited because I had been handpicked by the coaches, especially since, as I mentioned earlier, I had been a late bloomer and didn't have the Pee Wee/Pop Warner experience I assumed my teammates had. The high school coaches wanted a closer look at the young players coming up the following year. Our coaches told us it would be a wonderful experience. A player on the varsity team had a great nickname, and his family was friends with my family. His nickname was Bo Dee, and he played the strong safety/rover position. He was a hard-hitting player with a great personality. I watched him lay the wood on offensive players in practice. You could hear his thumping hits from the practice field to the elementary school, and when he made an impactful play, everyone celebrated by calling his name.

I had the opportunity to practice with him, and the time I spent with Bo Dee confirmed my love for the position of strong safety. I wasn't as nervous to be on the field as most kids would be with the upperclassmen because he was there. "When you're on this level, you gotta make a name for yourself," he had told me. I didn't know how it would happen, but I was willing to do whatever it took to make it happen. As a result, it happened one day in practice. I made a great play, sticking the running back hard, making the tackle, and then he fumbled the ball. It happened so fast, I don't remember hearing any noise or my teammates or coaches yelling and celebrating the play, but at the end of the play, (after I gathered my bearings), Bo Dee and the entire defense surrounded me to do just that. It felt good, and at that moment, I knew I could hang with the big boys. After practice, Jesse told me he could hear the hit from one end of the practice field to the other. I was happy Jesse was there to see it happen. He waited for me to walk home after practice as he always did. He lived a few blocks from my house. As we walked home, he talked about the play. Jesse described it and relived it, over and over again.

Jesse felt I needed a nickname. "Why?" I had asked. He told me when I made the play, my position coach and defensive teammates screamed out my name, and it sounded like my mom was calling me in the house to take a shower and go to church.

"It's okay to be known by your birth name, but it just doesn't fit you as a football player," he said. Jesse started spitting out names to fit my style of play, one after the other, and none fit. He asked me who my favorite pro player was. I told him "Hollywood Henderson" from the Cowboys. He said you can't take Hollywood. Then he asked me to name someone else. I said, "Charley Waters" from the Dallas Cowboys, He was a strong safety, and I liked him.

"Does he have a nickname?" Jesse asked.

"I don't think so," I replied.

"Don't worry," Jesse said. "We'll come up with something, and we'll come up with a nickname for both of us."

We tried name after name and never found any that fit us. During my sophomore year, just before spring football practice started, Jesse and I were hanging out watching TV at his house. We were watching the "Dukes of Hazzard." It was a popular show at that time, and we watched it often. Even though Jesse spent a few years in the Bronx and loved saying he was a city kid, I think spending some time in Virginia had left its mark on him. Jesse wasn't the oldest of his siblings, but he was the oldest son. His father was a truck driver and traveled a lot. Jesse was the man of the house when his dad was on the road. I saw Jesse's role as man of the house, and it was very similar to the character Uncle Jesse on the show. So I took my shot and called him Jesse-Duke, and he liked it. I asked him what he thought about "Bo-Duke" for me.

"No! You need something that will last," and he spits out "Bo-Dean," and I loved it. It was the way Jesse-Duke said it and the way I heard it. Jesse-Duke had a fast-paced Bronx accent mixed with a Virginia accent. I walked out of his house to go to my house and Jesse-Duke yelled out my nickname, "Bo-Dean!" It was music to my ears, and I knew it was going to stick.

Perry enjoyed my story, and he turned to Rich and asked him if he had heard my story. Rich hadn't heard the entire story behind my nickname, but he knew my legal name. Rich remembered Bobby Lambert, the equipment manager, calling my legal name out to pick up my equipment travel bag for our first game on the road the previous year. Rich was standing next to Bobby D. After my name was called, Rich spoke rather loudly, "Who the heck is that?" Bobby said, "Bo-Dean." Perry was dumbfounded that Rich didn't tell him during summer camp. Rich figured I would tell Perry when the time was right. I also told them something I didn't tell any of my other teammates. My mom had called me "Sweetness" from the time I was a little chocolate morsel, and as a young teenager growing up, my aunts called me "Garbage Can."

Perry asked, "Why garbage can?"

"Because I ate everything in sight." I was small and thin. I was trying to grow and gain weight because I thought it would convince my mom to let me play football.

TOPIC 39. BEYOND RACE

After establishing ourselves as roommates, we began to live our lives like the rest of our teammates and classmates. We settled into the football season, dated, hung out together, and enjoyed college life. "Big Country" began dating a beautiful girl named Morgan[1]*. They had met the year before and finally decided to date. She was sweet, kind, smart, and had a warm personality. I could tell the first time I met her that Morgan was comfortable around me, and she had no issues with JD or X-man. And that was important because as more people (my old crew) found out where I was living, there was going to be more brothers coming through our room door.

Perry met Audrey days after starting class. From the outside, they were a perfect match but on the inside, that match was not made in heaven. Audrey was from an especially wealthy family. I didn't know if she was born an aristocrat, but the way she carried herself, she could've been one. She was, without a doubt, classy, pretty, highly demanding, a little whiney, and spoiled. She spoke as if she grew up on the Main Line, and she drove a BMW. She didn't have a mean bone in her body, but she walked around campus like she was mad at the world. She fit extremely well into the Main Line reality and culture. Audrey was the odd one in our group, but Perry liked her, so we did our best to treat her like family. She really got along with JD, and maybe that also played a part in Perry and JD becoming good friends. We often teased Perry by saying he was going to marry a socialite.

I started seeing Roxanne around the same time my roommates started dating their girlfriends. She began her college career attending an HBCU, as I did. And that's the only thing we had in common regarding our paths to 'Nova. I wanted her to feel comfortable and confident while dating me, so I introduced her to my roommates and a few of my teammates. Roxy

---

1 *Name changed.

had experience attending a PWI because her high school was just that, all White. I felt her experience attending a PWI helped our relationship because that was one less thing we had to deal with while dating.

Roxanne was equally friendly and pleasant to any girl, Black or White, seen having a conversation with me between classes or at any time (in other words, she wasn't the jealous or the mean Black athlete's girlfriend type). Roxy didn't fit that negative stereotype—the angry Black girl description quietly talked about on our campus. And that was important because some Black girls were labeled and described as angry toward White girls who were friends with Black athletes.

As the older roommate, I'd seen the social climate and culture change on campus over time. I lacked the experience when it came to some multicultural or social issues based on my high school background. But my roommates and I were bold enough to take a deep dive into the semi-taboo topic of Black athletes dating outside our race. We were brothers from other mothers for life and there was no subject too hard or untouchable to talk about. The conversation began with my dating history at 'Nova.

I wouldn't say I was fortunate, but others did say I was lucky to find a Black girl to date because there were so few walking around the campus. I didn't limit myself to dating a 'Nova girl. With all the colleges and universities in our area, it wasn't impossible to find a Black girl to date. There were a few small pockets of Black communities along the Main Line in Bryn Mawr and Ardmore. Plus, there were other towns and cities nearby, from Norristown to Philadelphia. I was more than comfortable dating someone off campus. I told my roommates about the time I dated a Black woman close to my mother's age, and when my mother found out, she went ballistic. My roommates thought I was really cool after hearing that story.

It wasn't a crime for Black athletes to date outside our race on campus, but Black athletes had to deal with suspicions, assumptions, and rumors all the time. My roommates knew it because they heard them, too. And most of the rumors were closed-minded words quietly repeated from the past. It was almost impossible to be friends with a White female classmate without someone thinking that a dating or sexual relationship was involved. Some Black girls and White guys would ask me if I was dating a White girl if they saw me holding a conversation with her more than twice during the week. I felt it was a double standard because my teammate Bobby D. introduced me to Sonya Bryant (a Black girl) from Harcum College. We became great friends, and she was on our campus a lot with her female classmates, but no one questioned me about our relationship. I was friends with a lot of White female classmates—Michelle from Havertown, Tuny from Radnor, Provo from Connecticut (not Utah), and others. We had classes together or we met through others and our friendships began.

Big Country and Perry assumed I didn't date White girls because I was dating Roxy. But, one time, they did ask me if I would date a White girl if I had the chance. And I told them about the two (one Italian and the other Irish) that got away. The Italian girl was from Connecticut and the Irish girl was from Boston. The Italian girl was special. It was easy to be seduced by her smile, personality, and beauty. She was the first White female to show interest in me, but I didn't know how to deal with the potential relationship if it had gotten serious. The Irish girl was dating someone within her race. She was the sweetest girlfriend a guy could date. I'd run into her all the time, and it was if we had the same schedule. She was cool. She didn't come off as someone with money or uncomfortable around Blacks. Her boyfriend didn't treat her well. He broke her heart. A few of my friends and I wanted to go find him and teach him a lesson, but after calmer heads prevailed, we decided against it. She ended up leaving school. I kept telling myself it would have been a disaster if we had dated because it wasn't the right time for me.

In the meantime, and between those times, I flirted, teased, and partied with my White female classmates as most guys did. "Big Country" and Perry wanted to know which Black athletes dated outside their race. During my freshman year, there were a few upperclassmen athletes dating outside their race. From what I could tell, they were in good relationships. I could see how comfortable and confident they felt. They were unaffected by the social and cultural norms that held other Black athletes back from dating outside their race. Some Black athletes were frustrated and felt the pressure of being tagged with the accusation of selling-out, leaving, or turning their backs on their race, if they were seen publicly dating outside their race. So they kept their relationships secret for as long as they could. Maybe I was naïve and didn't see it as hiding their relationship because I was raised to never kiss and tell.

Perry wanted to know, "Do you feel any peer pressure to date within your race or be called out?" I had no issue with my identity as a Black athlete. I didn't need to pull out my "I'm Black card" to prove it. I knew who I was and where I was from. I didn't need to be reminded that I grew up in an all-Black environment, attended an all-Black high school, and would have stayed at the oldest HBCU in the United States if 'Nova didn't come calling my heart. Those immature antics didn't faze me. I didn't have time for it, and I shrugged them off. Now the residual effects of some of the Black athletes choosing to date outside our race left fewer options for the Black females on campus. The Black girls were already at a disadvantage because the numbers were not in their favor. We were students attending a PWI and there were more Black girls on campus than Black guys. So that meant, from their viewpoints, they had limited options.

I told Perry about one dating relationship I was aware of that didn't end well. During the '85 championship run, a Black basketball player was going through it with his White girlfriend. Their relationship ended. His head wasn't in the game, and his heart was being torn to shreds.

Every time I went to his room or even walked past his room, he was playing the song by Chaka Khan, "Through the Fire." I felt so bad for him because I knew what he was going through I had been there for a little while when the break-up happened with my girlfriend from Cheyney, but I quickly bounded back. However, I hadn't been there in the form of dating outside my race. By the time my roommates and I had our dating-outside-my-race conversation, I knew that relationships were complicated enough without throwing race in the mix.

CHAPTER VII

My Final Race

TOPIC 40. SWITCHED RACE

By the time my final college preseason practice in 1988 started, I was a senior and mentally ready to ride the bench and support my defensive teammates the way I was taught by my high school coaches and after hearing the best coaches in the country say it on TV. I knew what was in front of me. I was prepared to face it and take it like a man. I could see the light at the end of the tunnel, and that light was my future. I was twenty-three years old, eagerly ready (as most seniors, with a smile on my face) to accept that "White" paper with "Black" ink and move on to the next challenge in my life.

During warm-ups, the quarterbacks and wide receivers coach, Craig Johnson, approached me and told me that there was no position open for me on defense as a defensive back, and he would love to have me join the offense as a scout team wide receiver. As he continued to sell his idea of why it was important to the team for me switch to wide receiver, I felt like I had the wind knocked out of me . . . or worse, felt I had been gut shot. I remembered the conversation my high school coach had given me about sacrificing for the team, which earned me the FCA Athlete of the Year award, and so without hesitating, I agreed. I liked and felt comfortable with Coach Johnson because of our conversations over the years, and his wife, Meg, tutored me when I was having trouble with a few classes. He and Meg were always in my corner.

Although I wouldn't receive an award for sacrificing my personal dream to benefit the team, I realized my reward would be completing what I had started—finishing out my playing career with my teammates. I had built relationships and a reputation with teammates and acquired memories that would last for the rest of my life. I knew quitting was not an option for me, and I knew my teammates would respect whatever decision I made that day.

During practice, my teammates whispered to each other as I practiced with the offense. A few of my offensive teammates (Chris Seeger and Mark "Flute" Reilly) felt terrible for me but immediately stated how happy they were that I wouldn't be giving them sleepless nights anymore. Now it was time to dish some pain out to the guys on defense, and a few of my teammates on defense knew it was coming.

After practice, a number of my teammates approached me to voice their opinions. I responded, "I'm okay," but mentally and emotionally, I wasn't. I had to deal with my new identity as an offensive player and not the identity of a tough-minded defensive player I had created and earned on the field. I needed a day or two to figure it out. I'd dealt with many issues on campus as a student, an athlete, and a Black athlete, and I had worked through them all.

One way I was able to deal with the move to offense was through Rich and Perry. I was now on the same side of the ball as my former roommates.

A few days later, I headed to the Pavilion to check in with Mr. D. regarding my work-study job for the year. When I entered the Pavilion facility, I could see him from a distance as he walked into his office. Mr. D. had a concerned look on his face, and when he saw me, he immediately started yelling at me. He yelled, "Where were you? Where have you been? I haven't seen you in a few days!" Mr. D. had heard what happened (probably from Bob Lambert), and he thought I was going to quit the team. I told him I wasn't quitting the team.

"When have you known me to quit anything these past five years?" I asked.

Mr. D. asked me how it went down. I told him that my former position coach didn't have the courage to talk to me about the move. Maybe he thought I would quit and that was his plan during spring practice, to run me out of town. But what he didn't know was that there was no quit in me. "Not before he arrived, not while he was coaching me, and not ever," I said. I could have easily and cowardly used my Black identity and personality as a reason he rejected me as a defensive player. And maybe Mr. D. would have agreed with me just to help me feel better about the way I was treated, but that would not have been fair or provable. But I was levelheaded, and I'm glad I chose that path.

And then Mr. D. did what he'd always done after yelling at me or having a heart-to-heart conversation, but this time it was a little different, and it felt different to me. He stood up, grabbed his keys, and asked me to have lunch with him. Then, he said, "I'm proud of you. You've come too far to let anything or anybody stop you from finishing what you started."

At that moment, I remembered Mr. D. was a former Marine. And all the yelling and tough love he showed me from the first day I started working for him in the cage was because he was preparing me for the challenges I would face in college and life. I noticed he didn't ask me to close the garage door and lock it, nor did he ask me to keep up as he walked away, as he'd always done in the past.

Mr. D. was fine walking with me at his side. As we walked to his favorite place on campus to have lunch, I got the feeling this walk was different. It felt different. It never dawned on me that I should've stopped by his office to tell him how things were going or that everything was okay. For years, I watched sports on TV and heard athletes refer to their coach or mentor as a father figure. Over the years, Mr. D. had called me his adopted son or referred to himself as my surrogate father. And during our walk, I realized Mr. D. was more than a mentor, a high school football coach, and my work-study boss. I finally got it. Mr. DiCarlo was my father figure.

The first game of the season came quickly, and it was a home game. I was relegated to the bench, but I supported my teammates. The next two games were on the road, and I didn't travel with the team. I started to plan for parent's weekend because my mom would be attending. I didn't hide in my dorm on those weekends. I moved around campus as if everything was fine. When I was stopped and asked why I wasn't with the team, I replied, "It's not my year." After the team returned from our second away game, a buzz began circling campus that my old roommate, friend, and brother "Big Country" had caught a touchdown. By the time I made it to his room (a single in Austin Hall), his mom had called because she saw the highlights on ESPN. I could tell he was happy his mom had the chance to see him on TV. Although "Big Country" and I didn't live in the same dorm our senior year, we did our best to continue our Sunday chicken dinner run. We both looked forward to our moms meeting for the first time.

I talked to my mom and Irish twin a lot about my college experience over the years because I wanted them to live vicariously through me. My mom didn't know much about football, but she remembered me telling her how well I played during my third year. She remembered I played defense, and she remembered the day I told her I was moved to offense. And as most mothers do, she heard the disappointment in my voice. I tried to play it up as I always wanted to play receiver, but she knew that wasn't true. A few games later, it was parent's weekend, and all the parents of the seniors were there to attend the game.

It would be the only game my mom had the chance to see me in my blue or white Villanova uniform. At half time, all of the seniors escorted their parents onto the middle of the field, and a photographer took a picture of the players and parents. Each player and his parents were introduced to the fans. While the introductions were taking place, my mom whispered, "Sweetie, why were some of the parents around me saying they should put you in the game?"

I said, "Don't worry about it, Mom. A lot of my teammates' parents know me, and they were just being nice."

She said, "Some people yelled your name out."

"It's okay, Mom."

Then the PA announcer introduced my mom and me, and the crowd gave a really nice applause. She could hear people loudly calling my name, and that's when she realized that her son had lived his dream of playing college football.

Final Home Football Game, Senior Year. Ceola (Mom) and Bo-Dean Sanders

I made big plans for my mom's visit to 'Nova and Philadelphia. I spoke to Mrs. Erving, and she gave me tickets to the Luther Vandross and Anita Baker concert held at the Spectrum arena where the 76ers played their games. And I definitely had to take my mom to try a Philly cheesesteak at Mama's Pizzeria on Belmont Ave. before the concert. After the game, all the parents of the seniors gathered to meet the head coach outside our locker room. It didn't take long for me to get cleaned up because I didn't play more than a few plays, which was par for the course for players who didn't play during the season. I headed out of the locker room to find my mom. My head coach pulled me to the side to ask me a question. He told me my mom said something to him that he didn't understand, and he wanted to know what she meant by it. I told him I didn't know. My mom left him with a little nugget to chew on for a while and apparently, it hit home. My mom had the opportunity to do what every other parent "Black or White" had done for years. She complained about her son's playing time. We ended the season on a three-game losing streak, and the parting gifts for the seniors were our blue and white jerseys.

TOPIC 41. HATFIELD VS. MCCOY RACE

As I reflected on my time at 'Nova and started preparing for my future, I fully embraced my environment and appreciated the friendships across all cultures and ethnicities. I remember hearing the story about the "Hatfield's and the McCoy's" from one of my White classmates, either Tim McGuckin or Victor Miller. The story centered on a feud between the Hatfield family and the McCoy family in the Southern Confederate states of West Virginia and Kentucky. Two White families with hatred so big for each other that the legendary story lived on for decades. One thing was for sure—the two families killed each other as if it was a sport. I could relate to the feud and part of the story because I had lived through a bitter feud, a two-person rivalry.

It started as a personality conflict between one of my best friends, Veltra, and his teammate, Gary Massey. Gary was an outstanding basketball player. He was an incredible and all-world defensive specialist. But for some reason, Veltra and Gary didn't get along, and I wasn't shocked because I understood that not all Black people got along. I had learned at a young age that everyone in my Black neighborhood didn't like each other. After Veltra had transferred to another university (against my wishes), the animosity Gary had toward him transferred to me. Gary was a full-scholarship athlete. Gary Massy, Doug West, and Kenny Wilson were the three amigos who replaced EZ Ed, D-Train and Gizmo after winning the National Championship in '85. Everyone on campus hoped the three highly recruited players would continue the legacy of winning championships but that didn't happen.

At first, I was nice to Gary, as I was to all my classmates, Black or White, but there was something about him. I couldn't put my finger on it for a long time. Our relationship started as a prickly one and grew into a flat-out blood feud, but that was okay because I also knew that not all Black athletes were "homies" or best buds or brothers or equal members of the crew. He couldn't stand the same air that I breathed. He'd rather die of thirst and hunger than drink or eat in the same cafeteria. I thought Gary's attitude and disdain for me would get better over time, but it didn't. I assumed with so few Blacks on campus and since we were both Black athletes, he would find a way to at least try to get along with me. He was guarded and unapproachable (to most people). On the surface, he appeared to have a rigid and intimidating persona, but privately, he was a teddy bear, according to our mutual friends.

I was still learning things about people from different parts of the country. I became friends with and got to know many of my Black and White classmates from New York, and people from New York were definitely different. I learned that from dating my first girlfriend at Cheyney. They were tough, street smart, you couldn't hustle them, they had no time for BS, and they couldn't-care-less about your problems because they were from a city that had eight million of them. And Gary fit that description to a tee. Our mutual friends assumed it was personality differences because he was a Yankee, and I was a Southerner. We were like oil and water, and nothing, it seemed, was going to change it. Our North versus South feud wasn't about ownership of territory or states' rights or involved human beings. Our civil war wasn't going away, and one day it would reach a boiling point.

Most of our White friends didn't understand our issue. Our epic rivalry had many layers, and after I looked deeper into what our problem was, it became clear to me what part of our issues were. We clashed because we were cut from the same cloth. I was a few years older, but we were both born under the same zodiac sign, Cancer, the crab. And yes, we were crabby. Our birthdays fell in July, only thirteen days apart. Cancers can have two distinct personalities. We're very loyal if we like someone, and we could be friends for life, as long as that friend didn't screw us. We're very passionate regarding anything and everything we do. If we don't like you, your best bet would be to stay away. We have an evil streak. Some might say, "We've got the devil in us." We can be sensitive, caring, warm, and romantic. Gary and I were both mommas' boys and our relationships with our fathers were complicated. And finally, we protected those who needed protection.

When word around campus began circulating that we didn't like each other, that's when I knew it had come from him because he sold more Wolf tickets than the ticket master. Although I had a bone to pick with him, I didn't say anything to anyone on campus about how I felt. He was in a race to get more of our classmates on his side. At times, it made people around us uncomfortable and put them squarely in the middle. The dislike we had for each other was thicker than the humidity in Florida during the summer and heavier than all the concrete in the Bronx. If we happened to walk past each other, he would look at me with a sneer on his face, and I replied by turning my nose up at him. People couldn't understand why we didn't get along. If you asked most people that knew us both, each would say great things about us. Despite how much our friends tried to get us to tone it down and fix whatever problem we had, we couldn't do it.

The fight of all fights was going to happen and maybe it would happen before we walked off the campus for the last time in our caps and gowns. It didn't make sense for two Black athletes at a PWI having a beef with each other. A few of our teammates referred to the feud as Ali versus Frazier and if that was true, then I was Ali hands down. Our friends thought we were competing to be one of the BMOC (big men on campus), but I didn't feel that way because Mike Bamberger, a journalist from the Philadelphia Inquirer had already said as much in a news article about me: "Bo-Dean is a well-known figure on campus." I saved that article.

Honestly, I didn't have time to compete with Gary because I was always in survival mode as a non-scholarship athlete. Massey toyed with picking a fight with me for three years, but in his fourth-year sharing time on campus with me, our rivalry escalated beyond a feud, even though I had hoped a truce would be reached by our senior year.

His public image was not like other Black athletes on campus. He represented the Black athlete that, on the surface, held true to Black culture. Most of his Black teammates dated outside their race, but he was proud of the fact that he didn't. He wore it like a badge of honor. I completely understood how he felt and respected him for it. But I was past that way of thinking. There was no confusion or second-guessing where he stood on Black identity and dating. His longtime girlfriend was beautiful, smart, and possessed a wonderful personality. Everyone liked her. The brothers on campus who did date within our race were afraid to approach or talk to her because Gary intimidated them. Not me. I went out of my way to speak to her or say hello to her all the time. I think he saw it as disrespecting him, and that infuriated him, and I knew it. That's when our rivalry moved to bad blood.

Ultimately, we had to fight it out. It happened at the Al E. Gators sports bar and restaurant. Gators was our go-to spot for drinks. Although we were graduating in 1989, my senior classmates and I partied like it was 1999. Gary decided to show his cards and make the first move. We had words, and I decided to call him out because I'd had enough of his intimidating behavior during our years on campus. I like to say I'd, "had it up to my hammer" with him because there was only so much I could deal with from him anymore. He wanted to fight, and I was more than happy to oblige. It was fight-night and the moment of truth was in front of us both: It was go-time.

A flurry of fists started flying, and our friends tried to stop us. The fight went from the front of the venue to the parking lot. Most said the fight ended in a tie. After it was over, our very good friend, Vanessa Pressley became a casualty of war from our immature antics. She was slightly injured during the fight. Vanessa (loved by everyone) was the younger sister of Harold Pressley of the Sacramento Kings and our former classmate and Gary's former teammate. I remember the look of disappointment on Vanessa's face as the police decided whether to take us to jail or not. I felt regret and shame over the entire situation. We were reckless and had acted like knuckleheads. Before our fight, it didn't occur to me that one of our friends could have been seriously hurt from our stupidity.

TOPIC 42. FINISHING MY RACE.

While many of my classmates were contemplating their futures based on the job market, successful internships, family connections, and the university's reputation, I took advantage of the on-campus resources to find a job. I followed the advice of the Assistant Sports Information Director, Jimmy DiLorenzo, and signed up with the career development center and met with Director, David Leibig.

I started interviewing for my first career job after football. My growth, development, experiences, and evolution at 'Nova prepared me for interviews with a few of the top companies in the country. I was able to land multiple interviews with one of the largest wine producers in the country. I couldn't tell you if it was divine intervention, luck, or coincidence because my crew, classmates, and teammates knew one of my favorite adult beverages were wine coolers. I was known for drinking their product in my dorm room or out at the sports bars. I was known for drinking wine coolers because I wasn't a big beer drinker. And by the time my senior year had arrived, I had added champagne to my Sunday brunch routine.

I enjoyed the interview process, and I treated it like the football recruiting process. Each manger I interviewed with got the best from me, and they seemed to appreciate my energy. I had no interviews with anyone who looked like me, but it didn't matter. I was prepared for that. I had no chip on my shoulder or bad baggage I carried because in the end, I didn't let a few bad experiences with people who didn't look like me hold me back. I didn't fake my way through the interviews. I turned my baggage into luggage. I was confident and comfortable with who I was, and if a company's representatives weren't, then it didn't matter; I moved on without a problem.

The last few months before graduation were moving fast, and I had so much to do with so little time. On my list was: attending "Big Country's" ZETA PSI pledge party, personally hanging out like it was 1999, attending our football banquet (I looked forward to receiving my varsity jacket and ring), and the senior golf outing at Radnor Country Club (Big Country and I planned to play in the same foursome. If it was the last thing he did on Earth, he was going to get me to enjoy golf.) And finally, I had to complete the arrangements for my family's attendance at my graduation. The anticipation for the big day was building everywhere on campus. Everywhere I went, something exciting was happening. One afternoon, I was headed to "Big Country's" room to get the information about his fraternity party.

On my way back to my room, I came across a group of White students gathered in front of the Connelly Center. I assumed it was an on-campus fraternity and sorority group about to make noise about some up-coming event, but I was wrong. The group was staging a protest rally because of the injustices happening in South Africa. I had no idea what they were talking about, so I stopped to listen a bit longer. Everything said at the rally was over my head. I wasn't familiar with the name Nelson Mandela or the Anti-Apartheid Movement. One person after the other spoke (more like yelled) to the crowd in support of Mandela. I couldn't stay to listen to them all, but as I walked away, I remember gazing at the crowd one more time, and I noticed I was the only Black student there. I didn't think anything of it at the time, but I remember thinking I hope what they're doing helps the people in South Africa.

I wasn't a gifted athlete, and I knew it, but I had worked very hard. I was blessed to have friends and supporters on and off campus that believed in me. I was thrown a "Hail Mary" by one of my supporters. I clearly didn't have the end of my football career out of my head and heart. Over the years, the Erving family showed interest in my football career and me. Mr. and Mrs. Erving invited me over to their home to discuss my future. Mr. Erving talked to me about being aged out. He described how some players never get playing out of their systems. He'd seen guys put their futures on hold to chase their dreams and that could sometimes backfire. He didn't want that for me. He offered to use his contacts to get me in the supplemental combine, and I accepted his offer. The scout camp was held at Georgia Tech in Atlanta for undrafted college players eligible for the NFL draft. And that was perfect because my sister lived in Atlanta, which meant I didn't need to stay in a hotel.

On the day my acceptance letter arrived from the scout camp, my first job offer arrived from the wine and beverage company, as well. I could feel my heart beating through my chest. My emotions were racing a mile per minute. I was torn, more at that point than ever before because I believed I still had more football in me, and all I needed was one shot. I knew I had a small chance to make it, but I was reminded of the opportunity every time I saw Andre Waters from Cheyney University on the field in a Philadelphia Eagles jersey. So I decided to wait until after my pro football scout camp workout to decide on my job offer.

I arrived at the Philadelphia airport on time and made my way to the terminal for my flight. I was still uncomfortable flying. I was so focused on staying calm that I didn't notice who was seated next to me until he kindly asked me if I was a Villanova student. I turned to make eye contact and answer his question, and it was Tom Brookshier, NFL broadcaster and former player. He had noticed my 'Nova hat, which I had completely forgotten was on my head. We talked the entire plane ride. I was lucky to be seated next to him because he knew football and had forgotten more football than I ever knew. He was the nicest pro football legend I had ever met. I told him my story, and he was genuinely interested. We talked about my short time at Cheyney and about Andre Waters. During our conversation, I didn't blame my coaches for my college football career, nor did I make excuses for not playing my last two years.

All I wanted was a shot to see if I was good enough and Mr. Brookshier completely understood where I was coming from. I told him about my job offer and my plan. He offered some advice, and it was the perfect advice for me at that time . . . and very similar to Mr. Erving's advice. We arrived in Jacksonville on time, and as we waited to exit the plane, he asked me if I was driving to Atlanta. I told him my sister was home to visit my mom and she would be driving me back to her place. I told him my sister was driving me crazy because she had so many plans for me while in Atlanta. One of the last things he said to me was, "I'm sure your family is proud of you." I didn't want to intrude or be nosy, so I never asked him why he flew into Jacksonville. We shook hands and parted ways. I made it to Georgia Tech a few days later, and my sister dropped me off and wished me luck. I gave everything I had in me during the combine workouts and at the end, my letter grade/evaluation came back as a "C." And that was the end of my football career.

Two days before graduation, my family and friends arrived in Villanova, Pennsylvania. I wanted everyone to enjoy as much of the area, from Villanova to Philadelphia. Attending my graduation was my mom, Pam, and Pam's best friends, Tammy, Brenda, Carla, Caria, and one of my high school teammates, Troy. Everyone had a great time during their visit. At one point, while we were out eating, my mom asked me when I was coming home. I'm glad my sister and friends were there to tell my mom about my job offer in New York because I just couldn't. I could see the pride in her eyes, and I understood why she had hoped I would come home. She wanted to experience that motherly pride back home in our neighborhood.

After the graduation ceremony, we headed back to the dorm to relax before they all headed home. I kept an eye on my mom to see the smile on her face and the pride she displayed as we walked from the football stadium to the west end of campus (kind of a long walk). I introduced my family to almost everyone who knew me: one or two campus security guards, the staff in the bookstore (Mary and Sally the Irish sisters), Terry Susa and Tony Alfano from the Connelly Center, and any professors who happened to be walking by. I was lucky to run into Dr. Helen

Lafferty. If there was one person on campus who smiled more than me, it was Dr. Lafferty. I took her up to Jean Fazio's office to meet the woman that had worked so hard to look over and under every financial rock to keep me in school. When we arrived at St Mary's Hall, I pointed out to my mom the dorm I had lived in my freshman year. A few of my family members stopped to take pictures of the dorm and at that moment, we heard a car horn beep. We turned around to see who it was. To my surprise, it was Mrs. Turquoise Erving in her Mercedes 500 SL convertible. She yelled, "Congratulations, Bo-Dean. Is that your mother?"

I replied, "Yes, ma'am!" She said hello to my mom and family while forcing all the cars behind her to stop. And that was the brightest smile I saw on my mom's face during the weekend. So all the encounters and friendships I had told my mom about over the years had now been confirmed. And at that moment, my dreams and my final race became bookends.

Conclusion

My recurring nightmare started after I was arrested and had spent the weekend in jail on the Main Line. It was back in the early '90s, after getting into a fight with and seriously injuring two White guys. I was living in Hempstead, Long Island, New York (a.k.a. Strong Island). I traveled back to the Main Line (about a three-hour ride) often for special occasions. I had planned to meet my former classmates and 'Nova crew members at the Al E. Gator's Sports Bar and Restaurant for the St. Patrick's Day weekend celebration around 8:00 p.m. The main attraction at the sports bar was Charles Barkley of the Philadelphia 76ers. One day a week, Charles was a frequent guest on a local radio show held at the sports bar. Charles was friendly with most of the athletes in our "'Nova crew," and he often invited members of the crew to stop by and of course, we did.

Despite what anyone said or believed regarding Charles's off-court behavior, ninety percent of the time, Charles wasn't the problem at night. It was a small number (one or two) of guys acting out or behaving like schmucks or jerks in the local watering holes. They were the problem. The first guy was the typical, obnoxious mutant that invaded your personal space while you're trying to hold a conversation with someone, or he'd try to shake your hand while you're in the men's room, holding your manhood. The other dude is the beer-muscled idiot that gets out of control and starts doing something stupid. Both can't handle the watered-down liquor from their home or an adult beverage from a nice sports bar. And at some point during the night, they would start a fight with any athlete to make a name for themselves. Why? Maybe because of the jealousy or resentment they had toward the athlete . . . or any athletes. Both mutants weren't good enough to play sports on the college or pro level.

I expected to see a large crowd with their green T-shirts, beads, hats, and shamrock images tattooed or drawn somewhere on their bodies to celebrate St Patrick's Day weekend. As I walked into the sports bar, I remembered the last time I was there and how I had gotten into a fight with my college rival, Gary, and how I hadn't been in a fight since. Gator's was the first stop of the night before heading to the after-hours club called The Yorkshire, about a half-mile or so down the road in Bryn Mawr. I had experience participating in a pub-crawl during my years at 'Nova, and I wanted no part of that so two local spots were good enough for me.

The atmosphere felt different that night. It didn't have the exciting vibe it normally did. I'd had a long day, so I planned to pace myself, but the occasion called for lots of shots.

All night underneath the fun we were having, something in my gut told me it was time to "Katy bar the door" because it was going to be one of those nights, and I was right. At the end of the night, everyone decided to follow each other to the after-hours spot. Not me! I decided to walk and get some fresh air. The first thing on my mind was to stop at the convenience store to pick up some of the snacks I couldn't find in New York.

As I walked to the next party stop, I noticed a group of young Black high school girls traveling together, heading home, and I thought, "That's smart of them to travel in a group." I knew they were going home because a small pocket of Black families lived in the Bryn Mawr and Rosemont area. About one minute later, I heard a loud bang, the sound of a door aggressively opening and hitting the wall. I looked in that direction, and two White guys were running out of the door of a dive bar, and they were drunk. I didn't think twice about it, and I continued on my merry way.

Seconds later, I heard the girls scream. I looked to see what was going on. I saw the guys running through the young girls, knocking a few of them down on the ground and into oncoming traffic in the street. I had no proof, nor will I ever truly know how many pints of beer they had hoisted and chugged, but what I did know was they were downright giddy about calling these young Black girls horrible racist names. They seemed to enjoy the bigoted and dangerous behavior, inflicting harm on the young girls. In my mind, it was wrong, and I knew I had to do something about it.

I couldn't just let that happen without getting involved. I was raised to protect my sisters at all cost and to never hit a woman, no matter what. So my instincts kicked in. My intention wasn't to fight but to let them know they were being schmucks and what they did wasn't cool. After I said my peace, I thought it was over. But seconds later, they tried to bushwhack me. They assumed they had the drop on me, but what they didn't know was that I'd been in more than a few fights in my day. I had experience with being outnumbered and jumped before. I was ready! I thought it was either going to be an all-out brawl or a hilariously funny skirmish because three guys with enough alcohol in them to open a liquor store were trying to throw round-house punches.

I went toe-to-toe with two guys, one my size and the other two inches taller and bigger.

After I hit the guy my size, he dropped like a tree cut down by a lumberjack in the forest (it wasn't fair). Then, it was time to go at it with the guy who was bigger than me. In my mind, it was now a fair fight. It took a few extra punches before he was paying the price for what he and his buddy had done to the girls. As I stood over both guys, the girls screamed, "Run, get outta here!" I waited as they ran away. After all the girls were out of my sight, I decided to get out of Dodge and run. I didn't want to be that Black man on the run, but at that point, I was knee-deep in a bad situation. I ran to the after-hours club, and my crew was there. I spotted Buzz (the smart one) and as I approached him, I could see the concern in his eyes. He wanted to know what happened to me. I looked at my shirt and blood was everywhere. He pushed me into the men's bathroom and took off his sweatshirt. I ripped off my bloody shirt and put on his sweatshirt. The plan was to get the heck out of the club (and the area), and then figure out the rest later. By the time I had walked out the front door of the club, the police were there waiting for me. When it was all said and done, I was arrested, heading to jail, and the drunk guys were in the hospital. The police told me one would be fine but the other was touch-and-go. As I went through the booking process, I thought, "Was it a righteous fight, and should I have gotten involved?" My gut and heart said *yes*.

A few months went by as my attorney and I prepared for my court date. I often wondered if my Good Samaritan actions fell short or if my actions outweighed the bad outcome. The official ruling was for others to decide. However, I decided I wouldn't change a thing. I had done what I thought was right.

Two weeks before I was scheduled to appear in court, the two attorneys reached an agreement, and the charges were dropped. I assumed the two White guys had come to their senses and realized that a full court procedure would out them for their racist behavior, and they didn't want their family and friends to discover what they had done. The judge had some harsh and strong words for me but not for the two other guys. I was disappointed but not surprised. My actions were questioned but not theirs. I hoped the judge would've been impartial in the closing remarks (since no one had ruled me guilty), but that didn't happen.

I ended up running from this nightmare for years.

Acknowledgments

Writing this memoir was the second hardest task I have ever accomplished. You just read the first. I mention so many people in this book, people who played a role in my social development as a student athlete. Now, I'd like to acknowledge those people who played a role in the process of writing this book.

First, I must start with my sisters, dad, daughter, and other family.

My sisters—Pamela, Cassandra, and Alicia—and my dad, Joseph, Sr., thank you. Pamela Joyce, or PJ, who called to check on me and offered her professional contacts. My "Irish-twin," San, who's been there to listen and offer moral support. My baby sis Alicia Joann, or AJ, who wrote her book in four months—wow! It took me four years. (It's our running joke.)

My dad. I learned more about him, his music background, and his career while having conversations about my memoir.

My daughter, Mina. I love you today as I did the first second I laid eyes on you and held you in my hands. I wrote this book to help push this world toward a better place for you.

I want to tell the world that Sarah Ward Lage, "Queen of the Big Country," the wife of Rich "Big Country" Lage, has been my biggest fan, and I love you for it. And my brother from another mother, Richard "Big Country" Lage. Once again, you've been an amazing brother and teammate. The friendship and brotherhood I have for you is unbreakable. Although Perry Hodge and I haven't talked as much as "Big Country" and me after I graduated, Perry is no less my brother than the day I graduated from 'Nova. Thanks for returning my calls when you were busy at work. My heartfelt gratitude goes to Jessica and Eric Vassall (little E), my brother with the heart of gold and God. A profound thanks to my golfing brother, Michael Bivens, for allowing me to putt some ideas back and forth whenever there was time. I love you all.

As a member of the Delaware Country, Pennsylvania Press Club, I heard another author say my memoir is my second child. I agree, but I didn't give birth. I played a major role; however, my teammates, classmates, contemporaries, professional colleagues, friends, and frenemies made this story come to life. To my interns—Maria Mercedes Ktoan and Jaylen Pearson—many, many thanks for being patient with me from the start. To Rich Pagano, I appreciate your efforts to keep me moving when you were very busy with your sports column. A big shout out to Amanda Kulakowski Bruton, who was always available and willing to use her time and resources to help. Molte grazie to my PR team, Andrea DiFabio for her kind heart.

A special thanks goes to Delco Press Club members Peg DeGrassa, Andrea DiFabio, Annmarie Kelly, Doreen McGettigen, Marianne Rhodes, David Belanger, Adriene Irving, Cindy "Pony" Faiteich, Art Leagh and Tracy Price-Lochetto.

It is a privilege to know and thank my supporters: Carolyn Prante, John Durso, Jr., The Joy of Sox and Chief Sock Person, Tom Costello, Jr., John Beilenson, "The Magic Man," Howard "Poly" Polykoff and Bernetta Ayers.

Also, 'Nova nation members: Adrian Farris, Darla Wolfe, Wally Zimolong and Jim Cashman.

From the 353 Building: Jeff Larsen, Tim Roach, Eric Richman, Brandon LaMar, and Joe Ferguson.

RiSK ADVISORY: My guys, Andrew Addis, and Grant Phillips. An additional shout out goes to these great listeners Michael Croce, Jeff Sorg, Kristen Hubbert, Colin Raws, Pam Eitzen, Alicia Rhoden, Sarah Nuzzo, Tracey Johnson, Mr. Syd Goldberg, James Fletcher, and Mr. Joseph O'Shea.

Thank you to my photographer, Chuck Weems, Michael Curry, Esq., and my webmaster, Ed Rose.

I can't forget my Wawa crew: Marci, Ta-Nika, Lauren, Judy, Lauren, Kayla, Dom, Cindy, Alexia, Michael, Vicky, and Zac.

Finally, a "Good Deal" of thanks to Aubrey Kosa for referring me to my (superstar) editor, Cortney Donelson. Cortney was the perfect fit. Cortney provided additional suggestions and her insight was amazing. I immediately appreciated her experience, knowledge, and excitement. To David Beruh, thanks for connecting me to my publisher. And to my publisher, Morgan James Publishing. Thank you for being the only publisher out of many to believe in my binary narrative.

Most authors would never acknowledge the doubters or those who didn't believe in their ability, desire, strength, and confidence to write and complete their projects. However, those who know me know I'm one of the few authors that would do just that.

So to all those who love, believe, and dream with potential, energy, skills, support, and resources, please continue to do what you do best. Write! To those with love who want to believe and dream, don't quit!

Keep fighting, writing, and reaching for the stars. And to the doubters, the only thing I have for you is "God bless your heart." Enough said!

About the Author

B o-Dean Sanders was born in 1965 in Jacksonville, Florida where he and his siblings were raised by their single mother. He learned his values by attending his grandmother's Baptist church. His love of sports began while watching college football on Saturdays and NFL games on Sundays. Bo-Dean represented Jean Ribault High, his all-Black high school, as the Fellowship of Christian Athletes (FCA) athlete of the year in 1981–1982 in football. He started his college football career in 1984 as a walk-on at Cheyney University, the oldest

Historically Black College-University (HBCU) in America and then transferred to Villanova University, where in 1989, he earned his varsity letter and became the first male in his family to receive a four-year, Bachelor of Arts degree. Villanova had previously dropped football after the 1980 season but reinstated it in 1984. Bo-Dean began his football career at Villanova as one of five Black football players on the majority White team.

Bo-Dean is the founder and former president of BDS Marketing and was the general manager (GM) of an amateur, semi-pro, and professional sports arena, Tri-States Sports, home to the Philadelphia Soul, professional indoor arena football team, and Philadelphia Kixx indoor soccer team. He worked for Comcast Media in the Government & Community Affairs Division and held important roles with three non-profits: United Way, Urban League, and Blue & White Scholarship Foundation.

He's currently a member of the Delco Press Club. Over the years, Bo-Dean has been part of notable articles in the *Philadelphia Inquirer*, *Delco Times*, *Town Talk*, *Delaware Business Magazine*, *Out & About Magazine*, *County Press,* and *Main Line Today*. Bo-Dean writes about diversity & inclusion in sports and the positive impact multiculturalism had on his personal relationships in college.